PERSONALITY AND PERFORMANCE IN PHYSICAL EDUCATION AND SPORT

PERSONALITY AND PERFORMANCE IN PHYSICAL EDUCATION AND SPORT

by

H.T.A. Whiting, M.A., Ph.D., A.B.Ps.S.,
Department of Physical Education,
University of Leeds.

K. Hardman, M.Ed., M.A.,
Sub-department of Physical Education,
University of Liverpool.

L.B. Hendry, M.Ed., M.Sc.,
Department of Education
University of Aberdeen.

Marilyn G. Jones, M.Ed.,
Bedford College of Physical Education,
Bedford.

Henry Kimpton Publishers
London 1973

Standard Book Number 85313 781 1

I.B.M. Computer Typesetting by Print Origination, Liverpool
Printed by Unwin Bros. Ltd., Woking.

Acknowledgements

The editor and publishers wish to thank

Charles, C. Thomas, Publisher, Springfield, Illinois for permission to reproduce a figure from Eysenck, H.J. *The biological basis of personality.*

W.H. Freeman & Co., Publishers for permission to reproduce a figure from J.D French. *The reticular formation.* Copyright © 1957 by Scientific American Inc. All rights reserved

British Association for the Advancement of Science for permission to reproduce two figures from Gray, J.A. (1968). The physiological basis of Personality. *Advancement of Science,* 24.

Contents

INTRODUCTION

Within a psychological framework, personality theory is concerned with the nature of individual differences. Approaches vary, from the speculations of the armchair philosopher at the one extreme, to the semi-rigorous approach of the laboratory experimentalist at the other. A continuum might be proposed along which the various theoretical systems could be placed according to the amount of objective evidence produced in support of their contentions. Towards the more speculative end of such a continuum would appear the psychoanalytic approaches of Freud and the post-Freudians (Brown 1964) and towards the more scientifically derived end of the continuum, the work of psychologists like Cattell (1967), Eysenck (1967) and Witkin et al (1962) with which the overviews in this book are primarily concerned. In making these differentiations, it is not intended to impose value judgements on the validity or usefulness of one approach as compared with another. The bias in this book towards the suggested personality theorists, is a reflection of the amount of reported work in such contexts which might have implications for the student of human movement, physical education or sports psychology.

The literature relating to personality theory is vast and it is not difficult to understand why an interest in personality description, explanation and assessment has developed. Individual differences are a fascinating area of study for the amateur as well as the professional, providing a constant source of interest. At the same time, they can lead to much of the misunderstanding which exists both within and between different groups of people. Their everyday manifestation in social interaction situations necessitates at least some understanding of such differences if communication is to be effective.

Most theories of personality are based on general principles of behaviour which are characteristic of all or particular sections of a defined population (used in the statistical sense). That is, the presence of similar *traits*—consistent behaviour patterns over time—are apparent across individuals and that to some extent, laws of behaviour may be capable of formulation. While within a particular culture each personality is unique, people do tend to develop in roughly comparable ways. Individual behaviour as Allport (1955) suggests is mediated by common cultural upbringing and on this basis alone, communalities of behaviour are to be expected.

We are able to note consistencies in our own behaviour and we are able to note relatively stable behaviour patterns over a period of time in different individuals with whom we come into contact. We commonly use classifications in attempting to generalise about such behaviour. Thus, we might refer to a person as 'persistent' because in his individual acts of behaviour the quality of 'persistence' has been *consistently* observed or 'industrious' because he is *consistently* hard-working. This is not to deny the possibility of idiosyncratic forms of behaviour within such populations.

The word personality would appear to have derived from the term 'Persona'— the mask worn in ancient drama (Fordham, 1953). Such masks naturally enabled a person to appear to be something or someone other than himself. There is little doubt that people do wear a 'mask' (in this sense) in their everyday contact with the outside world and that if we assess a person superficially and within a limited context on what he *appears* to be, we are quite likely to be misled, for individuals play *roles* which may change under different environmental conditions. The dominant extraverted sportsman who is the life and soul of the entertainment after a game may be a shy, retiring individual within his own family setting! Nevertheless, a *biosocial* (Hall & Lindzey 1957) appraisal of personality is useful—particularly in everyday communication with people. We know on the basis of a common linguistic understanding what the person is trying to convey when he makes such as assessment and in any case, it is the 'mask-like' behaviour with which we have to contend.

Personality and Communication

Communication within a group is a social skill which as Argyle (1969) implies, is acquired in a similar kind of way to any other skill and can be represented by a similar model (Whiting 1969). Successful interaction depends in the first instance on an accurate 'reading of the display' (represented in such situations by the outward manifestation of an individual's personality, often in the form of posture, gesture or other movement behaviour). The outcome of such interaction is determined not only by the quick and efficient reading of such 'displays', but is affected by the individual's own personality, his knowledge of his own personality characteristics and the ways in which these are likely to relate to the personality characteristics of the individual(s) with whom he is attempting to communicate:—

> An individual judging others with respect to a given trait will be determined in his own judgement not only by objective reality, but also by his own possession of this trait. (Eysenck 1964).

It would appear, that the greater the insight the individual has into his own personality and into the personality of others, the more able he is to adjust his behaviour to the existing social environmental circumstances.

In making personality assessments in everyday situations we generally have to rely on *unstructured* situations, while in the more formal testing carried out by psychologists, assessments are generally based on behavioural responses to *structured* situations:

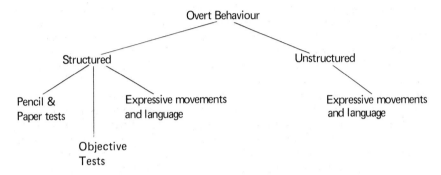

Personality Assessment

The following methods have been most often used in personality assessment:

1   Rating by others either in a structured or unstructured situation
2   Personality questionnaires or inventories—self-rating (structured)
3   Objective measures (structured)
4   Projective techniques (structured)
5   Life record (unstructured)

The use of pencil and paper type tests of personality and relatively static performance tests have become more or less standard experimental procedures, primarily because of their expediency in the testing of large samples. Their originators would be the first to agree that their usefulness is limited in unsophisticated hands and outside the normal clinical or experimental situation.

While the clinical interviewer would appear to be more inclined to take cognisance of the overt behavioural manifestations of his patient in the clinical setting, such assessments are limited in usefulness by their subjective nature. The expression of the emotions in terms of movement, posture and gesture is not a new idea. Darwin (1921) in the middle of the last century was one of the earlier workers in the field to consider such possibilities in man and animals. Vernon & Allport (1933) developed this work further but such procedures were little utilised. More recently, the possibility of using posture and gesture in man as an indicator of individual differences has been exploited by Lamb (1965) and North (1972). It is interesting for the student of human movement to speculate in this respect upon the possibility of using predominant modes of movement behaviour as a means of personality assessment, it being considered that in the adult subject these would constitute relatively stable measures.

It might have been expected that the study of the expression of personality characteristics in movement form—particularly in relation to communication where posture and gesture play such a significant role—would have formed an integral part of the training of students of physical education but this would appear to be the exception rather than the rule. Part of the difficulty lies in the limited attention and experimental investigation which has previously been given to the topic and the dearth of such interest shown by the people one would have expected to be primarily concerned with human movement.

Currently, there is an upsurge of interest in subjects such as 'non-verbal' communication, which promises to open-up exciting possibilities in many fields of study (Argyle 1969; Lamb 1965; Brooke & Whiting, 1973). Jones (1970) from the physical education field carried out a pilot investigation into the possibility of using assessment of 'effort' characteristics (in Laban's, 1960, terms) as a personality measure. Developments of this kind of approach are likely to follow.

Individual Differences in Skill Learning

It is apparent to anyone working in the experimental field of perceptual-motor skill acquisition that any general trends noted need to be qualified by drawing attention to the marked individual differences which occur. Eysenck (1966) is more specific on this point in suggesting that very often individual differences alone account for more of the variance in an experiment than the other variables on which the interest of the experimenter is focused. Unfortunately, there has been too little attempt on the part of workers in this field to deal adequately with these discrepancies.

It is not difficult to understand why such individual differences are present. Subjects come to any skill learning situation with different back-grounds of experience which will affect their skill development. They do not enter any situation as completely naïve individuals. They possess abilities which may differ in kind or degree (Fleishman, 1967) which have been established, by differing early perceptual-motor experience or by the interaction between such experience and genetic predisposition.

If the human organism is conceived as an information-processing system (Whiting, 1969), some of these ideas slot more easily into line. The physical mechanisms involved in such a human system are the sense organs, the brain and the effector organs which functionally perform the tasks of the input of information to the central mechanisms, the processing of such information and the carrying out of an overt or covert response. It would be wrong to think of such a communication channel in mechanistic terms as would be implicit in the acceptance of a strictly interpreted S-R psychology which conceives of the organism as being primarily reactive (Allport, 1955). Decision-making intervenes between the reception of information and the carrying out of a response. Even in that behaviour which might be classified as relatively habitual or pre-programmed, the decision has to be made as to *when* to initiate the response. Thus, the organism (O) as a personality intervenes between the reception of the stimulus and the carrying out of the response (S-O-R). The individual's prior experience of similar situations, his predispositions, his mental 'sets', his physique and many other personality characteristics will determine the kind of decisions that are made. In some situations, he may decide to take more risks than he would in others, or the level of risk he is prepared to take may vary in similar situations on different occasions. He may be concerned with the 'pay-off' which is likely to occur should he make one decision rather than another—some individuals play for safety others live continually on a knife edge.

Individual differences may play an equally important part in the reception of information and its transmission to the central mechanisms. These may mani-fest themselves as variations in the physical structure of the receptor mecha-nisms themselves which limit or extend the possibilities for information reception. Again, in order to take in information from the environment it is necessary to *attend selectively* to particular parts of the 'input' space. This necessitates a decision (in most cases) on the part of the subject to orientate his perceptual mechanisms in a particular way. Individual variations in such orientation are to be expected. Thus, the possession of differing levels or kinds of *schemata* in Piaget's (1952) terms, *analysers* in Sutherland's (1959) terms, *filters* in Broadbent's (1956) terms or *abilities* in Fleishman's (1967) terms together with differences in their hierarchical structuring would be expected to lead to marked individual differences in the way in which environmental information in any skill learning situation is treated.

In another way, individuals may have a bias towards one class of information rather than another where a particular situation provides input information on a number of different sense modalities (Wober, 1965). In addition, particular cultures may predispose their people to predominant modes of selective attention/perception such as Wober (1965) has recently illustrated. It is also possible that different child-raising practices between different sub-cultures may reflect differences in the value which is attributed to particular forms of sensory input.

Information from the environment is relayed in the form of electrical energy via the sense organs to the central mechanisms. Three subsystems may be usefully suggested here—the perceptual mechanisms, the translatory mechanisms and effector mechanisms.

The act of perception involves the bringing to bear of past experience on current sense data in an attempt to impose a meaningful structure. It is here that individual differences will play a predominant part. Differential experience leads to differential interpretation of similar sensory inputs. To some extent, it is true to say that 'we see what we want to see' (particularly in a social situation), rather than being completely objective. Similar comments might be made in relation to the translation mechanisms and the effector mechanisms but these will not be laboured at this point.

Individual Differences and the Nature/Nurture concept

While students of human personality may differ in the extent to which they will adopt a primarily genetic or a primarily environmental viewpoint, personality development is clearly the resultant of an interaction process between genetic predisposition and environmental opportunity. The fact that the course of development of the infant in utero is determined by its genetic structure and that it has undergone a period of environmental stimulation—albeit of a restricted nature—leads to the expectation that individual differences will be manifested from birth or even earlier. The latter comment would be supported by any mother of more than one child at an anecdotal level! It is reflected also in Bridger et al's (1965) contention that babies appear to differ temperamentally right from birth as shown for example by individual differences in sensory thresholds which would result in differential responses to stress or social deprivation.

Schaffer (1966) in his hospitalisation studies of deprivation, utilised an active-inactive continuum to differentiate between the amount of *spontaneous* activity shown by new-born and very young children. His thesis that relatively inactive children would be more prone to deprivation effects was supported and interpreted in terms of a lowered level of 'arousal' because of their relative inability to obtain an adequate level of changing sensory input without the stimulation provided by a member of staff.

Individual differences in the presence or efficiency of particular kinds of selective attention/perception mechanisms (analysers/filters/abilities etc.) has already been alluded to. Whether these are primarily genetically determined or the result of particular kinds and amounts of environmental stimulation is open to question. The work of Fantz (1967) in which the response of newborn infants to various arrangements of schematic facial features were charted led to the claim that some degree of selective attention is present in the neonate. Support for this contention comes from the work of Hershenson et al (1965) and Stechler (1964).

Since individual differences can be accounted for at least in part by genetic predisposition, it might be asked what form such predispositions might take? In as far as behaviour is mediated by glandular secretion and muscular contractions under the control of the autonomic and central nervous systems, primary emphasis must obviously be directed towards the structure and function of such subsystems. This kind of interpretation is particularly reflected in the work of Eysenck (1967) who has postulated a theory of individual differences in the following terms:—

> Human beings differ with respect to the speed with which excitation and inhibition are produced, the strength of the excitation and inhibition produced and the speed with which inhibition is dissipated. These differences are properties of the physical structures involved in making stimulus-response connections.

Eysenck (1967) relates such differences to his personality dimensions of extraversion/introversion and neuroticism and has produced evidence for the genetic basis of a person's standing on such continuua.

Eysenck's dimensions of personality have a bearing on the need for the individual to seek stimulation (and hence to indulge in greater or lesser amounts of movement behaviour); to enter into social situations and hence to use movement as a means of communication and to seek particular forms of physical activity or to restrict such participation to a minimum. The physiological interpretation of some of Eysenck's findings in terms of an excitation/inhibition balance and the concept of 'arousal' have particular implications for movement behaviour which are only just beginning to be made explicit. Some workers for example have pointed to the importance of kinesthetic feedback in 'arousal' terms (Bernhaut et al, 1953; Kulka et al, 1960). The degree of conditionability of an individual reflected by his relative standing on the extraversion/introversion and neuroticism dimensions has great relevance to movement behaviour in 'fear' situations e.g. learning to swim (Whiting 1970), rock-climbing, playing contact games etc. This concept needs further development at the present time.

The work of Cattell & Witkin

Cattell & Eber's (1964) sixteen personality factor analysis of personality characteristics has received considerable usage as a means of assessing particular criterion groups engaged in particular physical activities (see Kane, 1968; Hendry, 1970 for overviews). The higher-order factor derivatives of creativity, leadership and independence have significance but at this stage have not been greatly developed (but see Jones, 1970). The possibility of there existing stereotypes of particular forms of movement behaviour in criterion groups is beginning to be examined (Hendry, 1970; Jones, 1970).

The contribution of Witkin et al (1954; 1962) to personality theory has been through the medium of perception. They postulate a field dependence/ independence continuum related to the ability of the individual to separate figure from ground in perceptual tasks involving in many cases whole body participation and in others movement of a more limited nature (e.g. eye movements). The concept relates to hierarchical systems of information analysers which may be related to particular cultural pressures (Wober, 1965) and to particular forms of movement experience. In developmental terms, their concept of differentation/integration (Witkin et al, 1962) has implications for movement behaviour and the development of the body-concept.

Many of the implications outlined here, will be discussed in greater detail in the sections which follow.

Leeds October 1972   H.T.A. Whiting
                                                          Series Editor

References

ALLPORT, G.W. (1955). "Becoming." New Haven: Yale University Press.

ARGYLE, M. (1969). "Social Interaction." London: Methuen.

BERNHAUT, M., GELLHORN, E. & RASMUSSEN, A.T. (1953). Experimental contributions to the problems of consciousness. *J. Neurophysiol.*, **16**, 21-35.

BRIDGER, W.H., BIRNS, B.M. & BLANK, M. (1965). A comparison of behavioural ratings and heart-rate measurements in human neonates. *Psychosom. Med.*, **27**, 123-134.

BROADBENT, D.E. (1956). "Perception and Communication." London: Pergamon.

BROOKE, J.D. & WHITING, H.T.A. (Eds.) (1973). "Human Movement: a field of study." London: Henry Kimpton.

BROWN, J.A.C. (1964). "Freud and the Post-Freudians." Harmondsworth: Penguin.

CATTELL, R.B. (1967). "The Scientific Analysis of Personality." Harmondsworth: Penguin.

CATTELL, R.B. & EBER, H.W. (1964). "Handbook of 16 P.F.Q." Champaign: Institute for Personality and Ability Testing.

DARWIN, C. (1921). "The Expression of the Emotions in Man and Animals." London: Murray.

EYSENCK, H.J. (1964). "Sense and Nonsense in Psychology." Harmondsworth: Penguin.

EYSENCK, H.J. (1966). Personality and experimental psychology. *Bull. Brit. Psychol. Soc.,* **19, 62** 1-28.

EYSENCK, H.J. (1967). "The Biological Basis of Personality." Springfield: Thomas.

FANTZ, R.L. (1967). Visual perception and experience in early infancy. A look at the hidden side of behaviour development. In H.W. Stevenson, E.H. Hess & H.L. Rheingold (Eds.). "Early Behaviour Comparative and Developmental Approaches." New York: Wiley.

FLEISHMAN, E.A. (1967). Individual differences and motor learning. In R.M. Gagné (Ed.). "Learning and Individual Differences." Ohio: Merrill.

FORDHAM, F. (1953). "An Introduction to Jung's Psychology." Harmondsworth: Penguin.

HALL, C.S. & LINDZEY, G. (1957). "Theories of Personality." New York: Wiley.

HENDRY, L.B. (1970). A comparative analysis of student characteristics. Unpublished M.Ed. Thesis—University of Leicester.

HERSHENSON, M., MUSINGER, H. & HESSEN, W. (1965). Preferences for shapes of intermediate variability in the newborn human. *Science,* **144,** 315-317.

JONES, M.G. (1970). Perception, personality and movement characteristics of women students of physical education. Unpublished M.Ed., thesis—University of Leicester.

KANE, J.E. (1968). Personality and physical ability. Unpublished Ph.D. thesis— University of London.

KULKA, A., FRY, C. & GOLDSTEIN, F.J. (1960). Kinesthetic needs in infancy. *J. Orthopsychiat.,* **30,** 306-314.

LABAN, R. (1960). "The Mastery of Movement." London: MacDonald & Evans.

LAMB, W. (1965). "Posture and Gesture: an introduction to the study of physical behaviour." London: Duckworth.

NORTH, M. (1972). "Personality Assessment Through Movement." London: MacDonald & Evans.

PIAGET, J. (1952). "The Origins of Intelligence in Children." New York: Intern. Univ. Press.

SCHAFFER, H.R. (1966). Activity level as a constitutional determinant of infantile reaction to deprivation. *Child. Dev.,* **37,** 596-602.

STECHLER, G. (1964). The effect of medication during labour on newborn attention. *Science,* **144,** 315-317.

SUTHERLAND, N. (1959). Stimulus analysing mechanisms. In "Mechanisation of Thought Processes." London: H.M.S.O.

VERNON, P.E. & ALLPORT, G. (1933). "Studies in Expressive Movement." London: Macmillan.

WHITING, H.T.A. (1969). "Acquiring Ball Skill: a psychological interpretation." London: Bell.

WHITING, H.T.A. (1970). "Teaching the Persistent Non-Swimmer." London: Bell.

WITKIN, H.A., DYK, R.B., FATERSON, D.R. & KARP, S.A. (1962). "Psychological Differentiation." New York: Wiley.

WITKIN, H.A., LEWIS, H.B., HERTZMAN, M., MACHOVER, K., MEISSNER, P.B. & WAPNER, S. (1954). "Personality Through Perception." New York: Harper.

WOBER, M. (1965). Sensotypes. *J. Soc. Psychol.,* **70**, 181-189.

PERSONALITY AND PERCEPTUAL CHARACTERISTICS

by MARILYN G. JONES

Perception is always done by a particular person from his own unique position in space and time and with his own combination of experiences and needs. (Ittleson & Cantril, 1954)

Why perceptual modes should form an aspect of personality

Human behaviour is multi-stimulus determined. It is the resultant of a vast and complex interplay of interoceptive, exteroceptive and proprioceptive information impinging upon the brain and interacting with existing information stores within the brain itself.* In an attempt to simplify such a complex organisation, a model was outlined in the introduction with the primary aim of emphasising the important relationship which exists between input information and decision-making on outwardly manifested behaviour. Thus, at a simple functional level, three sub-systems were proposed:

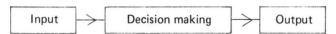

Decision-making involves choosing amongst competing alternatives. Audley (1970) has proposed two major aspects of choosing:

On the one hand, there is an active aspect involving a competition between alternative courses of action under the direction of prevailing motivation. In what is now rather outmoded terminology, this could be called the conative side of choice. On the other hand, we have the collection of information about the available alternatives which it would still be

---

* . . . the eyes, ears, nose, mouth and skin have been classified as exteroceptors; the end organs in muscles, joints and the inner ear have been called proprioceptors; and the pressured nerve endings in the visceral organs have been called interoceptors. (Gibson, 1968).

11

fashionable to label as the cognitive aspect. Obviously these two aspects can never be clearly separated; the cognitive processing of information is permeated by conative variables; there is often an active search for a basis upon which alternatives are to be compared and the collection of information is rarely a passive matter.

The latter statement reiterates Gibson's (1968) point about the human organism being an active seeker of information when the senses are considered as *perceptual systems*. Audley's statement, although having wider implications, makes the distinction between choice on the 'input' side and choice on the 'output' side and at the same time draws attention to the rôle of motivation in such choices. In this section, primary emphasis is on the 'input' side of performance—the selection of particular information from amongst the vast amount of potential information available to the *perceptual systems* (in Gibson's terms). In so doing, it will be neither possible nor desirable to ignore selection on the 'output' side nor to ignore motivational variables, but these will receive only limited treatment.

Individuals differ in their ability(ies) to deal with input information and in the categories of information to which predominant attention is given. Thus, a consideration of *selective perception* and dominant modes of information-processing constitutes a valuable and worthwhile aspect of personality study. If such perceptual systems can be shown to be relatively stable at particular stages of development then the ability to assess such systems in a qualitative or quantitative fashion represents a useful indicator of personality.

In view of these comments, it is surprising that little attention has been paid to such dominant 'perceptual modes' in specialist groups of people. In the present context, sportsmen, physical educationists and dancers particularly come to mind. But in spite of the extensive work of Witkin (1962) and his colleagues into personality through perception, relevant studies have been few.

One of the most important concepts related to both 'input' and 'output' information processing is that of *selective attention*. Because of the structure of the sense organs, the limited channel capacity of man, (Welford, 1968) and the sheer amount of potential information in the display, it is necessary for man's attention to be selective. This means that attention must be directed either consciously or unconsciously to specific areas of the display (or in Moray's, 1970 terms 'input space'). Knowing what information in the display is worth attending to will depend on the past experience of the person in relation to the skill that is being performed. In the educational context, it will be observed that one of the requirements of the good teacher is that he be aware of the important information in the display so that he can help the learner to make his attention selective. The ability to make attention selective in certain ways may be illustrated by reference to field dependent/field independent perceptual modes described by Witkin et al (1962).

Field-dependence/field independence.

Over the past twenty five years Witkin and his colleagues have been concerned with the nature of individual differences in perceptual behaviour, and in particular, with the consistency of such differences in certain situations. Their original studies suggested two polar extremes of perceptual ability, namely field-dependence and field-independence. In a field-dependent mode of perceiving, perception is dominated by the overall organisation of the field and there is a relative inability to perceive parts of the field as discrete. Conversely, in a field-independent mode of perceiving, parts of the field are experienced as separate from the organised background and not fused with it.

By investigating in greater detail the nature of the differences which were manifested by persons situated at different positions along such a field dependent/independent continuum, Witkin et al (1962) found themselves approaching the study of personality through perception: not only did their subjects show perceptual differences but also other personality differences.

Cognitive Style

Witkin et al went on to observe behaviour in other psychological areas which they hypothesised would relate to perception. It became evident from their findings that an individual tends to bring with him to many situations a certain approach within which is a consistent manner of dealing with a wide variety of perceptual and intellectual tasks. This characteristic approach of the individual they designate his *cognitive style* defined as:

> the consistent modes of functioning which characterise him (the individual) throughout his perceptual and intellectual activities. (Witkin et al 1967)

It also became evident that differences in cognitive style could be observed with reference to the perceptual characteristics people exhibit:

> Perception may be conceived as articulated in contrast to global if the person is able to perceive item as distinct from organised ground when the field is structured (analysis) and to impose structure when the field has little inherent organisation (structuring). Progress from global to articulated which comes about with growth, occurs not only in perception but in thinking as well. (Witkin et al 1967).

This global/articulated cognitive style dimension is of some interest and will be developed in a later section. The importance which is attached to such a concept is reflected in Broadbent's (1971) recent comment:

The techniques now available for describing cognition are ripe for application to this field, and the accounts of cognitive style and dimensions of individual variation will probably be the forerunners of many future developments.

Differentiation and Integration

Central to Witkin et al's present work is the concept of 'differentiation':—

Psychological differentiation has served in our studies to conceptualise particular consistencies observed in diverse areas of a person's psychological functioning. (Witkin et al 1968)

Thus, articulated experience is indicative of developed *differentiation* in a cognitive sphere, where *differentiation* refers to the complexity of structure of the psychological system of the person. Thus a less differentiated system, as Witkin points out, is in a relatively homogeneous state, whereas a more differentiated system is in a relatively heterogeneous state. It is important to stress the use of the word relatively, for even the most simple system is differentiated to some extent. Integration refers particularly to:—

. . . the form of functional relations among parts of a psychological system and between the system and its surroundings. (Witkin, 1965)

Assessment of Field-dependence

Most of Witkin et al's work has been based on three main tests of field dependence/field independence; the tilting-room/tilting-chair test; the rod and frame test and the embedded-figures test. Each of these three experimental situations requires the subject to separate an item from its context, the item may be the subject's body, a luminous rod or a geometric design. Thus the style of perception which enables the subject to differentiate objects from an embedded background is designated by Witkin et al as field-independence.

1   The tilting-room/tilting-chair test

The apparatus for this test consists of a chair which can be tilted to the left or right which is placed within a small room which can also be tilted to the left or right. The test is in two parts, the body adjustment test (BAT) and the room adjustment test (RAT). In the eight trials of the room adjustment test, the room is tilted through 56 degrees and the chair 22 degrees. The subject's task is to adjust the room to the upright position while his chair remains tilted. In the six trials of the body adjustment test, the room is tilted 35 degrees and the chair 22 degrees and the subject must this time align his body with the vertical while the room remains tilted. The subject's score for each test is the mean degrees deviation of the room or chair—whichever has been adjusted—from the true upright when he reports it to be straight.

2 The rod and frame test (RFT)

The subject sits in a dark room and adjusts a tilted luminous rod which is centred within a tilted luminous frame to a position which he perceives as upright; meanwhile the frame remains tilted. The scoring system is similar to that which is utilised in the tilting-room-tilting chair test and is the measurement of the mean deviation of the rod from the upright. The practical problems of administering the rod and frame test, although not as great as those of the tilting-room-tilting-chair test, were still sufficiently inconvenient for Oltman (1968) to devise a portable rod and frame apparatus. He wanted to eliminate the need for testing in a dark room so that the apparatus could be transported to subjects instead of requiring the subjects to come to the laboratory. The apparatus which resulted is described by Oltman (1968):—

> A headrest is placed at one end of a rectangular enclosure which serves as the frame, and which can be tilted to the left or right at an angle of 28 degrees. The walls of the enclosure are of translucent plastic, and the tilting rod is visible at the end of the enclosure opposite the headrest. The subject's view is restricted to the interior of the enclosure by means of a curved shield which is attached to the headrest. Between the trials a curtain is raised in front of the subject's face to block completely his view of the inside of the enclosure. The base (24 x 36 ins) and the discs (22 ins diameter) forming the ends of the enclosure are of ¾ inch white acrylic plastic sheets . . . The enclosure rests on rollers in such a way that it can tilt smoothly to either side. . . . In general the apparatus was constructed so that no marks, screwheads or other irregularities appear on the inside of the enclosure or on the black frame which surrounds the rod, so that no cues are available to the subject which might make his responses artificially consistent.

Oltman then subjected his apparatus to tests of validity, using it alongside the standard RFT and the embedded figures test (EFT). The results (from 163 college students) showed the scores on the portable test correlated 0.89 with scores on the standard version, and there were no significant differences in correlations between the EFT and the two types of RFT (0.56 for the standard and 0.60 for the portable). In view of these high correlations, Oltman recommends the portable RFT as a valid substitute for the standard apparatus, and he further mentions the advantage that testing time is considerably reduced as no dark adaptation period is required.

3 The embedded figures test (EFT)

The embedded figures test requires the subject to detect a previously seen simple geometric shape drawn within a complex shape designed to conceal it. The test consists of 24 pairs of simple and complex figures and the subject's score is the total time taken to find each of the simple figures. Some people can locate the simple figure very quickly and their perception is designated field independent; others find it difficult, and some cannot isolate the simple figure even within the five minutes allowed; their perception is field dependent. A disadvantage of this test is the time involved, for it could take a field dependent subject over two hours to complete the test. Jackson (1956) has put forward a 12 item shortened form of Witkin's EFT, with a 3 minute time limit, and he claims that this gives a very good approximation of the results obtained from the entire test, while requiring only half as much administrative time. In order to select the 12 figures, he took a sample of 50 students, and selected 13 from each extreme of the field dependent/independent scale. The twelve items which most significantly discriminated between these extreme groups were included in the shortened form test. Alternatively, Witkin suggests that the test can be shortened simply by using the first half of his original order of 24 items. Reliability data for the shortened form of the EFT has been provided by Loeff (1962) and Karp (1963)—Table 1.

Table 1 Reliability data for short form of EFT

Investigator	Group	N	Method	Reliability Coefficient
Loeff (1962)	College men	100	Corrected odd-even	0.88
Karp (1962)	College men	100	Tryon's variance	0.86

These tests—particularly the Rod and Frame test and the Embedded Figures Test—have been used extensively in investigations of perceptual modes. Results of projection personality tests, the Rorschach, Thematic Apperception Test and Figure-Drawing tests, enabled Witkin (1949) to report indications that field-dependent subjects were greatly affected by pressures and standards of their surroundings both socially and environmentally. They were said to be relatively passive, to have a poorly developed sense of self identity and hence to be immature, to readily submit to authority, and to be anxious to please and conform; they were also found to be group dependent to some extent and to favour occupations involving other people. On the other hand, the field-independent person was found to base his actions and judgements on his own internal feelings and convictions and was said to be active, socially independent and in the extreme, aloof and almost cool.

It is of interest here to mention the work of Gardner and his colleagues (1960; 1961; 1962). They suggest that a single classification such as Witkin's field dependent/independent continuum could not give sufficient scope for an adequate description of the wide variety of perceptual characteristics and personality qualities that are apparent in human performance. They considered that Witkin's field dependence/independence dimension described just one aspect of a person's behaviour: it could not be the all embracing concept that Witkin conceived it to be. Gardner & Long (1962) prefer the designation field-articulation, and suggest that this is manifested as the ability to direct attention to significant aspects of the display and to ignore irrelevant aspects; in fact as selectiveness of attention. They included this field-articulation concept as one part of a much broader classification of an individual's make-up which they called 'cognitive control'. This would appear to resemble Witkin's 'cognitive style', but Gardner's field-articulation is a much narrower and more clearly defined concept than Witkin's field dependence. The link between field independence and selective attention which is supported by Gardner's contention will be considered later in this chapter.

Perceptual Continuua

Witkin et al's approach to personality has identified a continuum of perceptual modes, designated field dependence/independence. Results of other experimental work carried out on individual differences in perception have classified the different modes of perceiving in a similar way as pairs of contrasting types representing extremes of continuua. There are many such continuua, but no single one seems to give a comprehensive description of all the variations of perceiving. The following are examples of such continuua, but it is important to realise that each pair of perceptual modes represent extreme ends of a continuum and individuals take a position somewhere between the two extremes:—

Synthetic	— Analytic (Vernon 1970)
Objective	— Subjective (Messmer, 1904; Netschajeff, 1929; Smith, 1914)
Confident	— Cautious (Bartlett, 1932)
Sharpeners	— Levellers (Klein, 1951)
Form bounded	— Form labile (Klein & Schlesinger, 1951)
Extraverted	— Introverted (Eysenck, 1967)
Reducers	— Augmenters (Ryan & Kovacic, 1966)
Field dependent	— Field independent (Witkin 1949)

The last two categories of field dependence/independence and reducers/augmenters have particular relevance in a physical education context; the latter will now be considered further.

Reducers/Augmenters

Ryan & Kovacic (1966) felt that the ability to tolerate pain might be related to the type of activity in which a person took part. Their experimental work indeed showed that:—

(a) contact athletes tolerated most pain
(b) non-athletes tolerated least pain
(c) non-contact athletes fell between these extremes.

There are several explanations of these results, but one which appears to be the most appropriate is that the relationship between pain tolerance and type of athletic ability might be due to differences in a general perceptual characteristic of 'augmenting' or 'reducing' sensory inputs. Petrie (1960) has shown that some individuals will consistently reduce the intensity of their perceptions while others will tend to augment the intensity. On the basis of her work Petrie has identified three perceptual modes:—

(a) *the reducer*, who is tolerant of pain and tends subjectively to decrease what he perceives
(b) *the augmenter*, who tends to be intolerant of pain and subjectively to increase what he perceives
(c) the third type is *the moderate* who falls between the two

It is also of interest to note that 'reducers' describe themselves as alert, cautious, clear thinking, conscientious, dependable, determined, dreamy, efficient, enthusiastic, impatient, individualistic, industrious, intelligent, leisurely, modest, obliging, organised, practical, precise, quick, relaxed, self-confident and tactful.

The 'augmenters' describe themselves as bossy, careless, imaginative, logical, loud, sensitive and serious. It has been suggested that Petrie's 'reducers' and 'augmenters' are simply descriptions of extraverted and introverted personalities. But, Petrie is suggesting that a person's perceptual characteristics are the *cause* of introverted-extraverted behaviour.

The suggestion that the more extraverted person has a high 'arousal' threshold (Eysenck 1967) may explain their tolerance of pain which has given them the identity of 'reducers'. Similarly, the more introverted person with a low 'arousal' threshold will perceive pain quickly, and may appear to augment the intensity of the stimuli.

From the material discussed so far, it would appear that studies in perception and personality have considerable overlap. But as yet the nature of this overlap has not been clearly defined or explained. Individual differences which do occur in perceptual abilities have been generally observed in the *speed* and *accuracy* of performing perceptual tasks. It is difficult to separate the factors which contribute to performance on such tasks. Differences in speed and accuracy have, for instance, been explained as functions of heredity and experience (Eysenck 1967). It is also suggested that many of the tasks involve intelligence and past experience. Edwards (1968) found that perception was influenced by:—

1   Properties of the stimuli
2   Prior information about the stimuli
3   Method of testing
4   Properties of the senses employed
5   Motivation of the observer

and he points out that in an experimental situation, factors (1) and (5) above are external to the subject, (4) is innate, while (2) and (3) can be influenced by experience.

Investigations into the effects of training perceptual performance provide conflicting results. In many cases, training failed to produce any general improvement in range and accuracy of perception (e.g. Gibson, 1947) but work done by Renshaw (1945) goes counter to these findings, and Bruce & Low (1951) give partial support to the usefulness of training. In a review of experimental work in this field, Vernon (1970) suggests:—

> where some improvement has been shown, it probably results from improvement to direct attention towards particular aspects or details of the forms presented which facilitate their discrimination and identification.

thus providing further reinforcement to the importance of selective attention/ perception as an aspect of the perceptual process. For this reason, the following section attempts a closer study of the psychological and physiological aspects of selective attention.

Selective Attention

Eighty years ago James (1890)—one of the earlier investigators into the phenomenon of selective attention—had this to say:—

> Everyone knows what attention is. It is the taking possession by the mind in clear and vivid form, of one of what seems several simultaneously possible objects or trains of thought. Focalisation, concentration of consciousness are its essence. It implies withdrawal from some things in order to deal effectively with others . . . We cannot effectively deal with more than one thing at a time . . . unless the processes are very habitual, but then only two or three without very much oscillation of the attention.

He demonstrates clearly the importance of selective attention by further comment:—

> Millions of items of the outward order are presented to my senses which never properly enter my experience. Why? Because they have no interest for me. My experience is what I attend to. Only those items which I notice shape my mind—without selective interest experience is utter chaos.

It would appear, therefore, that only a small part of the display or 'input-space' (Moray 1970) is actively perceived by an observer. Generally speaking, the *successful* information is that which is considered important or interesting or else is that which the observer has been told to look for, but there are also other determinants. The fact that only some of the information gets processed is partly explained by reasons already quoted at the beginning of this chapter and partly explained by the limited capacity of the channels in the nervous system used to transmit information. Early in the century, Sherrington (1906) observed that sensory fibres are about five times as numerous as motor fibres, thus implying an inevitable bottleneck in the information processing systems. Berlyne (1969) elaborates this point:—

> There have been several attempts to compare the amount of information that enters the sense organs with the amount that is given out by effectors. Different methods of calculation have produced somewhat different results, but it seems clear that far less than 1% of the information taken in by the nervous system is able to exit through motor processes.

So the bottleneck is even more severe than Sherrington suggested. There seem to be a number of factors influencing the effectiveness of selective attention. Some of the more important are:

(a) Arousal level
(b) Expectation and set
(c) Habituation
(d) Distraction
(e) Stress
(f) Individual differences
(g) Novelty of stimulus
(h) Orientation reaction

(a) Arousal level

The concept of arousal is outlined on pages 104-111 in relation to Eysenck's (1967) introversion/extraversion continuum. It was suggested that there is an optimum arousal level necessary for effective task performance. A similar idea would seem to be necessary for *attention* to be maximally successful. This can perhaps be explained in physiological terms. It is thought that the diffuse cell network within the brain-stem and thalamic reticular systems has two main functions with regard to perception:—

1 Impulses from the brain stem reticular formation are capable of producing general cortical arousal on a continuum from sleep and passivity to alertness and excited states.
2 The thalamic reticular formation gives rise to a more persistent and localised response, sometimes called the 'orienting reflex' in which attention is directed towards particular kinds or sources of stimulation.

Degrees of attention to environmental information depend on both of these mediating mechanisms. Firstly the person must be alert (tonic arousal), and secondly the perception of significant aspects of the environment will be facilitated if sensory impulses related to such stimulation are reinforced by the thalamic reticular formation discharge (phasic arousal). Thus it is suggested that the reticular formation may operate in man to arouse the cortex and to direct excitation towards it in order to stimulate attention to information which is of particular significance.

(b) Expectation and set

It will be helpful if the person has some idea of what he will perceive in the display and for what he needs to search. The more precise this information, the more rapid and accurate his perception is likely to be. He is aware of what to expect and may be said to be 'set' to perceive particular aspects of the situation. In the games context, it would be expected that the experienced player will be the one who directs his attention quickly to relevant information, whereas the beginner will be attempting to respond to too much of the display and will waste time by processing information which is unecessary to the task in hand.

(c) Habituation

When a monotonous stimulus is repeated at frequent intervals, attention to that stimulus is decreased—this is the phenomenon of *habituation.* An example would be the ticking of a clock which attracts attention on first entering a room but quickly fades into the background. Thus, if a situation is repeated too many times, habituation may occur resulting in decreased arousal and failure in attention. Perhaps this is a case for repeating a manoeuvre in a game situation such that the defence get tired of the same tactic or, 'set' to expect it. A *new* manoeuvre will then have greater 'surprise' value (in an information theory sense) and hence will require a greater amount of time on the part of the opposition to deal with such novel information.

(d) Distraction

Among the factors which can adversely affect attention are distraction and stress. If stimuli are presented that are irrelevant to the main task, attention to the main task may be distracted. It will be recalled that field-dependent persons are greatly affected by distraction, whereas field-independent persons are more able to ignore irrelevant stimuli and direct their attention to the important information (e.g. EFT test). It has been suggested that distraction may well occur when the main task possesses little intrinsic interest. On the other hand, if the observer expects irrelevant information to occur, his attention to the main task may be increased and a better performance result. This could be illustrated by spectator cheering or booing at football matches—or indeed at any sporting event. The whole art of deception in games contexts is that of confusing the display in such a way that an opponent is misled. A deliberate attempt is made to draw his attention to wrong or redundant information in the display.

(e) Stress

Under conditions of stress the effect of distraction increases. Easterbrook

(1959) has found that in stressful situations observers tend to ignore certain aspects of the display that they would normally have noticed, and suggests that there is a narrowing in the range of cue utilisation: thus attention is in some way funnelled.

(f) Individual differences

Investigations into the effects of stress caused by sensory deprivation on perception have shown individual differences which are often fairly consistent. Generally, calm, placid and less intelligent persons were least affected, and where conflict in results did occur it is thought they might be attributed to differential effects of social isolation. Studies by Schaffer (1965) showed that effects of social isolation on young children were such that the developmental quotients of a 'hospitalised' group (the more deprived) were significantly lower than those of a 'baby-home' group (a group of children in an institution with a relatively high staff-child ratio). It was later observed that this was only a temporary decrement in performance for when the hospitalised children returned home, their developmental quotients soon rose to the level of the other group. The fact that social isolation has a more adverse effect on inactive than on active infants—in terms of the amount of spontaneous behaviour displayed (Schaffer 1965)—would support the contention that social isolation has differential effects which may be mediated by particular personality traits. Differential effects of stress might be accounted for in arousal terms by the Yerkes-Dodson law (Broadhurst, 1959). Thus, for every task an optimal level of arousal for efficient performance is proposed but this level varies for different individuals. Extraverts for example have been shown to have a higher threshold of arousal than introverts (Eysenck 1967).

Similarly for every performance there will be a threshold level of tolerance for stress, and this will vary for different individuals. Petrie (1960) has suggested that athletes tend to reduce sensory stimulation and will therefore have a higher level of tolerance for stress than would a non-athlete on a corresponding task. This could be illustrated by an experienced professional footballer who is regularly subjected to the stress of match play, whereas a newcomer to such stress might be considerably affected.

(g) Novelty of stimulus

Novel stimuli are more likely to capture attention than more familiar stimuli, because they will have a fairly high 'surprise' value (in information theory terms) and less opportunity will have occurred for habituation.

(h) The orientation reaction

The orientation reaction is derived from the term 'orientational reflex' introduced by Pavlov. When in operation this reflex causes animals to:—

immediately orientate their appropriate receptor organ in accordance with the quality in the agent bringing about the change making full investigation of it. (Pavlov, 1927)

Hence the orientation reaction refers to responses like head or eye movements or pricking up the ears so that the sense organs are focusing on certain environmental features. These responses are overt, and in the orientation reaction are accompanied by covert changes such as electroencephalograph (EEG) and physiochemical changes in the sense organs and also changes in muscle tonus. Fellows (1968) discusses two main functions of the orientation reaction:—

1 to increase the organism's capacity to extract information from the environment
2 to prepare the organism to respond on the basis of what it receives

Thus, the orientation reaction is important in both 'input' and 'output' stages of information processing.

Some of the factors influencing the effectiveness of selective attention have been outlined. The major problem, however, is to discover how the selection of material is brought about and where or at what stage in the perceptual process it occurs. Much of the research has been directed towards clarifying these problems, but results are not always in agreement.

Welford (1968) has suggested that selection could occur in two ways:—

1 where the classification process is carried out only as far as is necessary for the task under consideration i.e. specific details are disregarded unless particularly required
2 where certain classes of incoming data are filtered off at a relatively early stage in the perceptual process.

The concept of FILTERING has been utilised in all the theories on selective attention so far put forward. Broadbent (1958) originally proposed a filter between the sense organs and the central mechanisms. In this way unwanted information could be 'blocked off' without reaching the central processes. He points out that information travels along many input channels and since the central processing system has a lower capacity for information than the combined capacity of all the input channels, it could very easily become overloaded. In order to prevent this, Broadbent suggested that information from one input channel only is accepted for processing. This means that there must be a filtering system prior to processing, and discrimination of messages for allocation to channels must occur at a very early stage.

More recent work suggests that the filter mechanism is more complex than Broadbent originally postulated. Also, in view of Moray's (1970) contribution, the concept of a 'channel' would now appear to be somewhat misleading.

The relatively simple experiment of playing two messages simultaneously over a loudspeaker system has been used as the basis for many investigations, subjects being required to attend to one and ignore the other. Certain factors facilitated this difficult task:—

1   if the intensity or pitch of voices were different
2   if the physical characteristics were different
3   if the voices were separated spatially (stereophonically or over two loudspeakers)

and the clearest separation was obtained by playing the two messages separately into the two ears. When subjects were required to attend to one message only, it was found that they could recall little if anything of the other. But, in certain instances parts of the unwanted message got through. Usually these were words which were appropriate to the wanted message or else words which were very familiar to the subject (e.g. his name) or sometimes very unusual or interesting words.

Treisman (1969) carried out further experiments in the hope of extending Broadbent's work. She concluded that, since some of the unwanted information did get processed, the filter merely weakens (attenuates) rejected information rather than completely blocking it. Also, although difficult to define the exact nature of the separation, Treisman considered that it was obvious that there must be some kind of analysis of the data before the rejection is made. Her first model described two main events:—

1   Information analysed according to physical characteristics and then appropriately channelled
2   Accepted information passing through a selected channel and other channels carrying only important or novel information.

Treisman also proposed that words are stored in a kind of cerebral dictionary:—

There would have to be a stored memory of all known words against which to match oncoming signals since they could not otherwise be recognised. We need some kind of dictionary in the brain corresponding to words or phrases. (Treisman, 1969)

In such a procedure of input recognition, any input will activate certain units (words or phrases) provided that the input is of sufficient intensity to overcome the threshold for that unit. It is suggested that thresholds of units will vary and may be permanently lowered for important messages so that they are given ready access through the filter. Thus the idea developed at this stage would indicate that the filter distinguishes messages by their physical characteristics and the dictionary unit process deals with the content.

In contrast to Treisman, Deutsch & Deutsch (1963) suggest that information is not filtered until *after* perception. Thus all messages reach the perceptual mechanisms and are then segregated and interpreted. They contend that each message has a pre-set 'weighting' and the most important will initiate a response, i.e. they propose a *response* filter.

Further experimental work by Treisman & Geffen (1967) to support their earlier contention that information is filtered before perception was queried by Deutsch & Deutsch on grounds of validity. The problem of exactly 'where' the filtering takes place is as yet unresolved.

In 1969, Norman attempted to explain selective attention in terms of its relationship with perception and memory. He introduced a new concept of *pertinence* which appears synonymous with Deutsch & Deutsch's (1963) *weighting*. Thus, information is transported to the storage system where each stimulus is matched with a stored representation and the stimuli with the highest pertinence value are selected. The process of locating and recovering these stored representatives is called *retrieval* and the information obtained may be used in a response such as remembering.

Sometimes the stimuli need to be presented in a number of different ways (i.e. recoded) before the correct item can be recovered from storage. Novel stimuli give rise to new cues so that new information can be integrated into the storage system. If the stimulus is familiar the cue will have become established, perception will be improved and the response will occur if the pertinence value is high enough.

Moray (1970) neatly summarises his impressions of theories of selective attention when he suggests that such limited knowledge is presently available that no one theory can be completely right. Thus:—

> I do not underestimate the heuristic value of such theories, but a critical appraisal of the field strongly suggests that we know far too little yet to attempt to construct theories of the complexity which have been seen in recent papers. All current theories are probably wrong and none of them has really been adequately described by its proponent.

Analysers

An analyser is a cell or group of cells within the brain which only fires in response to a particular class of information (e.g. colour, sound wavelength, angle of inclination of lines, kinaesthetic information from muscles or from joints etc.). Treisman's most recent work (1969) suggests that there are three kinds of selective attention, each at a different level in the nervous system:—

1   Input selection, where the class of sensory data to be used is selected
2   Analyser selection of possible responses
3   Test or target selection within the analysers which leads to specification of responses

Audley's (1970) two major aspects of choosing which were put forward at the beginning of this chapter also distinguish between choice on the input side and choice on the output side. It would seem that the type of selective attention used will depend on the complexity and variety of the stimuli. Treisman suggests that the analysers may be arranged in series, parallel or else in a hierarchy where there could be two levels of analysers, one perhaps for the analysis of discrete stimuli and another for the classification of groups of stimuli. This possibility of a hierarchy of perceptual analysers is of great interest. (For a recent attempt to develop a model of perception in terms of a hierarchical organisation the reader is referred to Forgus, 1966). Also, the microelectrode studies of Hubel & Weisel (1959) have given considerable physiological support to this type of model in which perceptions are developed through a hierarchy of operations. From the results of experimental work, Treisman found that analyser selection is used predominantly for selective attention of single items and this occurs comparatively rarely. Nevertheless she claims that all types of selection are essential for a complete analysis of stimuli.

Welford's (1968) conclusion after reviewing experimental evidence on selective attention may link with Treisman's concept of a hierarchy of analysers: he suggests that there must be two filtering processes or else the peripheral must be explained away by the more central; alternatively it might be possible to have one filter with various stages.

Thus it seems true to say that a person may acquire predispositions to attend to certain classes of sensory input. Such predispositions may be influenced by training, expectations, instructions or just general interest. Failure of attention may be due to stress or distraction or to over or under arousal; in persistent cases it may also be caused by physiological deficiences of the nervous system. Successful attention is likely to be facilitated by an effective orientation reaction, optimum arousal and an ability to process information rapidly, which in turn depends on the person's ability to direct his attention to relevant stimuli. The actual process of selective attention may involve a hierarchy of perceptual analysers.

Fellows (1968) has discussed the hierarchical structure of sense modalities put forward by White (1965). His theory is based on the cognitive development of the child and the three levels suggested can be related to progressive stages of development. Thus input information is gained at levels:—

1 by visceral and interoceptive receptors (very young child)
2 by tactile and kinaesthetic receptors (young child)
3 by auditory and visual receptors (older child)

Schopler (1964) was able to show a progressive increase in the proportion of time spent in visual play as opposed to tactile play as children got older. He points out that a young child always likes to explore a new object by touching and feeling it, whereas an older child will be content just to look at it; this observation would appear to support the contention of a hierarchy of sense modalities and changes in the relative positions within such a hierarchy in the course of development. It was also noted that when presented with a complex task, the older child supplemented his visual information intake with tactile and kinaesthetic modes of perception. In Fellow's terms therefore, it would seem that individuals who predominantly use level (3) can also make use of lower levels to gain additional information if they so wish.

Zaporozhets (1957) reported a direct relationship between the amount of spontaneous orienting behaviour practised by the child and the efficiency of the final performance; this would suggest that effective performance can be encouraged by participation in orienting behaviour. The point can be illustrated by a study carried out by Neverovich (Zaporozhets, 1957) who showed that the efficiency with which tool operations were mastered and the actual standard of their execution were considerably higher when orientation to the method of performing the action could be produced in the child in the course of training; instead of the children's attention being directed towards the end product (i.e. getting a nail into a piece of wood), it was directed towards the 'feel' of the movement by getting them to hammer on a table in which the end result was of less importance.

Fellows (1968) has explained orienting behaviour as that which serves to clarify the relevant aspects of the task or make them more distinctive. However its main function as seen by Zaporozhets (1957) is to facilitate discrimination at a level which would be relatively low in Treisman's hierarchy:—

> . . . its main function is in the formation of the sensory part of the elaborated motor system in the preliminary analysis and synthesis of the afferent stimuli in the system.

Another interesting study utilising a hierarchical concept of perceptual modes was carried out by Wober (1966). He suggested that some individuals are predisposed to use some senses more than others for their information seeking.

While this has already been mentioned in connection with Fellows' (1968) investigations in terms of ontogenetic development, Wober points out that because of cultural influences, physical deficiencies or other effects, people have different predominant modes of perception. Thus blind persons will depend primarily on auditory perception, but will have developed kinaesthetic perceptual modes to a far more sophisticated level than a normally sighted person. Wober's work was not concerned with physically handicapped people however, but with typical populations in cross-cultural studies. He observed that certain African tribes relied almost entirely on kinaesthetic information, whereas neighbouring Europeanised Africans used mainly visual information. Some of his tests involved a version of the 'embedded figures test' which had been adapted to measure kinaesthetic perception—the shapes and patterns of the geometric figures were raised against a flat background, hence they could be identified either by feeling or by looking. Wober gave his subjects the normal instructions for the embedded-figures test and then observed the methods of solving the problem which the subjects employed. It was apparent that some relied very strongly on the tactile senses moving the finger over the patterns, while others did not feel the test cards at all. These results led Wober to suggest the existence of a predominant mode of perception in individuals. If this is true then it would appear that each person may have his own individual hierarchy of perceptual modes. It was observed that the subjects who used a predominantly kinaesthetic perception tended to have had little, if any education, and the subjects who preferred visual attention were relatively better educated. This again links with Fellows' hierarchy, which it will be recalled is based on cognitive development, but contradicts Schopler (1964) who showed that retarded children prefer visual play as much as normal children of the same age indicating that progression is more closely related to chronological age than mental age.

The work of Wober puts forward a most interesting proposition and opens up many possibilities. It may be that not only cultural influences affect an individual's predominant mode of perception, but also social or environmental influences i.e. such differences may not only be cross-cultural but sub-cultural as well. Certain occupations demand mainly reading, some require astute auditory perception, others involve individuals in physical activity. Is the predominant mode of perception determined by these occupational influences or are they counteracted by a sophisticated education which has developed and used visual perception so extensively? In the context of this book, one thinks of professional dancers, sportsmen and possibly actors and actresses. Of these, dancers might be expected to have a particularly sophisticated kinaesthetic perception for they consciously use the whole body in their movement. The work of Gruen (1955) is of interest here. She wanted to determine whether individual differences in spatial orientation and perception could be verified in a special group of people such as dancers. She suggested that one of the objectives in training dancers is increased sensitivity to bodily sensations and that this is achieved by providing training in muscular awareness and kinaesthetic sensitivity. The results of her work were not conclusive. It is observed that this statement was made some fifteen years ago, and the issue still awaits further clarification.

Ego-autonomy

Further studies indicating the usefulness of a hierarchical concept of perceptual modes include the work of Rudin (1968). He has observed some ambiguity in Witkin's work and suggests that the ability to separate the perceptual field into parts is not the same as the ability to perceive an object as distinct from its context. Rudin thus poses the question:—

> Is field independence a preferred mode of response which can be changed if the person is motivated to do so, or is it more of a habitual way of responding that the person will inevitably use whether or not he wishes or is motivated to do so? Is field independence a preferential style or is it an ability?

Relating this to Witkin's concept of differentiation, Rudin wonders whether a person can switch backwards and forwards from an articulated to a global perceptual style. The studies of Rudin & Stagner (1958) did indeed put forward a more flexible and general concept to explain Witkin's results. This was designated 'ego autonomy' representing the ability to direct one's attention to any aspect of the display and to decide for oneself what part of the display shall be figure and what shall be context. It would allow the person with an articulated cognitive style to switch to a global mode of perception if he so wished. This suggests a hierarchical system where field-independence is the predominant perceptual mode but individuals are able to switch to field-dependence if they so wish. In a ball game situation the switching mechanism of this nature might be illustrated as follows: the player is required to be aware not only of where the ball is, but also of the whereabouts of the other players and boundary lines of the pitch. It could be argued that a field-independent person quickly spots items as distinct from their context, i.e. where the ball is and what is happening around it whereas the perception of the field-dependent person would be influenced by the background, lines of the pitch etc. In order to be able to cope with all tasks, a person who can switch from field-independent to field-dependent perception as required would appear to be at a distinct advantage in games situations.

Personality and Perceptual Characteristics of Women Specialist Physical Education Students

Jones (1970) reports one of the few pieces of research work undertaken in an attempt to relate perceptual and personality characteristics. The criterion group comprised women specialist students of physical education. Her subjects (N = 140) completed a battery of perceptual and personality tests. The results from the perceptual tests (rod and frame test and the embedded-figures test) were compared with performances of other populations on the same tests, and it was shown that these physical education students showed a generally field-independent mode of perception. In view of the literature reports that women are more field-dependent than men (Witkin et al. 1962), it is interesting to note that these women physical education students were very similar to a group of American men students and more field-independent than a group of American women. Results from British populations are beginning to become available and follow a similar trend. Male physical education students in one study were more field-independent than general course male students, although differences were not significant (Hendry, 1970). Recent analysis of an international men's hockey team showed that this group tended to be more field-independent than all groups previously mentioned. These findings are of particular interest in view of the earlier discussion on selective attention (page   ).

Jones (1970) retested her subjects on all tests after a 9-month interval and the results showed significant changes in perceptual performance on both EFT and RFT (p < 0.01). The move towards greater field-independence is noted with interest. Some evidence in the literature has suggested practice effects in learning to analyse the embedded figures (Jackson, 1956) although test-retest reliability coefficients are high—0.88 (Loeff, 1962) and 0.86 (Karp, 1963). Many of the subjects who took part in this experiment voluntarily admitted to remembering some of the figures, and this may be due to the above average intelligence of the sample (mean for Otis IQ = 116). While it is feasible for part of the improvement in EFT performance to be attributed to practice and memory, it does not seem that this can account for changes in the RFT scores. It is suggested that by the age of 19, an individual will have reached a stable level in perceptual development (Witkin et al, 1967). It was postulated that movement education would have a direct effect on the body-concept and that differential experience in terms of dance, games etc. might have differential effects on such development. Draw-a-person test-retest scores did indicate an increase in the level of sophistication of body concept over the academic year, but the difference was not significant. The EFT and RFT scores, however, were significantly different (p < 0.01) and Jones attributed the discrepancy between these results and those on the draw-a-person test to the weaknesses in the test: she questioned the validity of the draw-a-person test as a measure of sophistication of body-concept.

A further analysis was made of the effects of different movement education programmes (i.e. dance or games stressed) on perceptual performance, but differential effects were not observed at this stage (19-21 years). Jones points out that such effects may have been disguised in the experimental work under consideration as all subjects had previously experienced a basic course in physical education which included games, dance and gymnastics. She suggests it would be interesting to investigate the effects of different movement education programmes on the perceptual development of younger children. Future studies with younger age groups may reveal the usefulness of devising remedial compensatory movement education programmes for children with perceptual difficulties or personality problems. If these speculations are correct, then their implications give movement education a very important role in the perceptual development of children and hence in the educative process.

Perception and Personality—further analysis

Warburton (1969) has suggested that

> Personality is built up by two main influences
> 1 the attempts made by a person to adapt himself to a changing environment, and
> 2 his efforts to change the environment, i.e. by adaptation and thrust. This element of give and take is highly important in the formation of those tendencies to react to the environment in certain ways which we call personality.

This contention arose from Warburton's structure of personality factors where higher order factor analyses on the sixteen personality factor inventory data (Cattell & Eber 1964) yielded two third-order factors. Warburton designated these factors 'adaptation' and 'thrust' and observed that individuals high on adaptation are said to make successful attempts to change their environment. Each factor combines two second-order factors, one of which refers to personal qualities while the other reflects attitudes to the society at large. A fourth order analysis gave two orthogonal factors (intercorrelation 0.00) of integration and morality. The factor of integration indicates overall success in dealing with the environment, for it combines successful adaptation to the environment (third order factor *adaptation*) with successful attempts to change the environment (third order factor *thrust*). Warburton also notes an important feature of this analysis, for morality appears to be a fourth order rather than a second order factor as had been assumed before the higher order analyses were carried out (Table 2).

Table 2 Warburton's personality structure based on Cattell's 16 PF

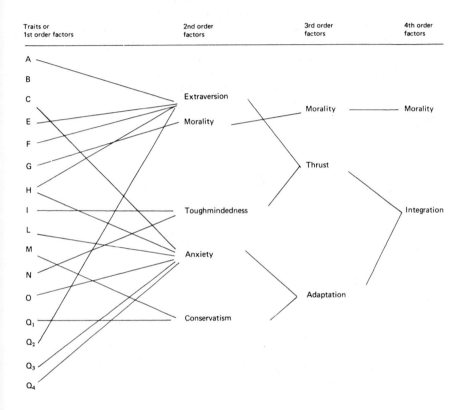

Cattell's higher order analyses

Cattell has isolated eight second stratum factor scores (Table 3) from the 16 PF primaries, all of which are described in detail in the 16 PF Handbook (Cattell & Eber, 1964). With this second order analysis of primary scores Cattell also obtains measures of *creativity, leadership* and *neuroticism*. Cattell discusses his third order factors as follows:—

These factors would not necessarily be expected to be personality factors in the ordinary sense, but rather influences in society or in the genetic background which effect some patterning in personality traits. The first which we have called strength of the nervous system, after Pavlov and Teplov, would be a favourable influence which encourages both exvia and cortertia. The second seems to derive from an influence favouring self criticism, possibly reflecting heavy parental authority. The third is a high responsiveness and alertness to the environment, as opposed to subjectivity and internal feelings, which might be temperamental and genetic. The fourth (a large contributor to the super-ego but one which negatively affects independence) could be a strong religious or cultural control effect and shows concern about one's values. The last indicates a form of serenity and detachment, with intelligence that could conceivably express a higher social status effect.

Table 3   Cattell's personality structure

1st order (16)	2nd order (8)	3rd order (5)
A B C E	Exvia	
F G	Anxiety	Strength of nervous system
H	Cortertia	
I		Self criticism
L	Independence	
M		Responsiveness to
N	Discreetness	environment
O		
Q_1	Prodigal subjectivity	Serene intelligence
Q_2	Intelligence	
Q_3		Morality
Q_4	Super-ego strength	

It would appear that the 'alertness to the environment' factor may bear some relationship to Warburton's third order factors of thrust and adaptation to the environment.

The concept of yielding—contending has been utilised in descriptions of human performance. Bauermeister et al (1963), in considering performance on the rod and frame test, designated persons who were field dependent, 'yielders' because they were influenced by—they yielded to—the position of the frame, whereas those with a field independent perceptual style who disregarded the influence of the frame i.e. who fought against it, were called 'contenders'. In a similar way, Warburton's two groups as described by his 3rd order factors were 'adaptors' and 'thrusters'—they yielded to their environment or fought against it. In movement analysis, Laban (1960) uses the terms yielding/contending to describe the attitude of the person which determines the quality of his movement.

Studies by Jones (1970) attempted to discover whether the yielding/contending concept was an underlying factor which could link perception, personality and movement behaviour, but while there did seem to be a connection, the nature of the relationship was not well defined. Table 4 shows the sten scores of women specialist physical education students on the third order factors.

Table 4 Sten scores of PEW on 3rd order factors

3rd order Factor	Mean	S.D.
Strength of nervous system	6.21	2.98
Self criticism	5.06	1.52
Responsiveness to environment	5.73	1.91
Serene intelligence	6.00	2.05
Morality	4.00	2.19

It is interesting to note the high score on Factor III (responsiveness to the environment) and also to observe the high but not significant correlation of 0.16 between this factor and scores on the Rod and Frame Test. A principal components analysis of the perceptual and personality test results is given in Table 5. The component which is of especial interest in this context is the eighth component which has loadings from the rod and frame test, and 16 PF factors M-conventionality, and Q_2-group dependence. For the purpose of her study Jones (1970) designated this factor 'yielding' because it suggested that a person is influenced by external realities—by the frame, by convention and by the group. It is interesting to note that the EFT does not load significantly on this factor; it has already been reported that the EFT and the RFT have about 20% of their variance in common, and this factor would appear to be concerned with the ability measured by the RFT alone—this might link with Bauermeister's 'yielding' concept.

Table 5
Principal components analysis : Perception and personality
(components tentatively named) PEW (Jones, 1969)

	Exvia	Unemotionality	Super ego Strength	FD	Tough minded ness	Discreteness	Independence	Yielding	SBC
	I	II	III	IV	V	VI	VII	VIII	IX
Eysenck's E	+85								
F	+86								
A	+32				−69				
E	+74						+31		
Q$_2$	−46							−38	
H	+74	+34							
O		−79							
C		+56							
Q$_4$		−83							
Eysenck's N		−84							
Q$_3$		+31	+62						
L		−38	−44	−32					
I			−47		−43				
G			+77						
Eysenck's L			+32		−48				
EFT				+87					
RFT				+71				+39	
N						+87			
Q$_1$							+84		
M							+35	−69	
SBC									+93
Variance	14.86	13.3	8.45	7.22	6.50	5.86	5.73	5.18	5.14

    Eysenck (1961) gives strong support to a view which recognises the existence of two clearly defined and highly important dimensions which have been called Extraversion/introversion and Neuroticism respectively. As already stated, physical education students tend to be significantly more extraverted than other students. Also, results based on two samples only show physical education students to have a generally field-independent mode of perception. If Witkin is correct when he suggests that field-independent perceivers have a more sophisticated body concept (for it is observed that his longitudinal studies used EFT and

RFT to measure development of body concept) then the findings of Jones (1970) and Hendry (1970) lend support to the reports of Sugerman & Haronian (1964) who noted that the tendency of the more mesormorphic and extraverted person to take part in exercise leads to a more sophisticated body concept.

An investigation into the relationship between personality dimensions and sophistication of body concept was made by Whiting & Johnson (1969) in their analysis of the results of tests of field dependence/independence, sophistication of body concept (HFD) extraversion/introversion and neuroticism (Eysenck) on 50 ten year old school children. Their results showed the relative independence of all four dimensions (Table 6).

Table 6 Personality and body concept (Whiting & Johnson, 1969)

	1	2	3	4	5
1 Human Figure drawing					
2 Embedded Figures Test	0.41*				
3 Extraversion/Introversion	−0.17	0.08			
4 Neuroticism	0.07	0.09	−0.14		
5 Lie Scale	0.18	0.17	−0.09	−0.04	

$* p < 0.01$

Whiting & Johnson suggest that a move towards greater field independence with age might suggest a change in the relationship between the dimensions being considered from childhood to adulthood.

Several other investigations have related Cattell's or Eysenck's personality theories with Witkin's field dependence/independence dimensions. Evans (1967) using the Maudsley personality inventory and the Embedded Figures Test reported a correlation of 0.39 between field dependence and extraversion. Bound (1957) found no relation between field dependence/independence and Eysenck's neuroticism dimension. The relationship between Witkin's concept of field independence and Cattell's second order factor seem to be associated in some way, but the nature of their relationship is not yet clear. Ohnmacht (1967) queries this link as low correlations were obtained in his studies. He states:—

It seems doubtful that the 16PF produces a referent of the construct field independence.

Johnson et al's (1969) investigation shows a stronger relationship between Q IV and field independence than did Ohnmacht's results but they support Ohnmacht's indications that Q IV is not a good questionnaire measure of field independence. Jones shows that field independent subjects do score more highly on Q IV than do field dependent subjects, but the difference is not significant (Table 7). Thus the findings do not really show any constructive evidence one way or the other.

Table 7 Comparison of Independence scores for FI and FD subjects (Jones, 1970)

	N	EFT		Independence		F	t
		M	SD	M	SD		(separate variance)
Group 1	24	187.3	52.5	6.62	1.4	2.70*	1.44
Group 2	22	1123.1	287.4	5.80	2.3		

*$P < 0.01$

Conclusion

Results of some of the available studies have been reported, and it is observed that there are very few of these. No doubt with the new possibilities that have merged from work of such people as Rudin (1968), Wober (1966), Fellows (1968) and Berlyne (1969) greater clarification will follow.

Perhaps the most important concept that has been discussed in this section is that of 'selective attention', for its effectiveness is crucial to the success of many kinds of athletic performance. Too often the perceptual aspect of skill is neglected while the performer concentrates on the technique of, for example, hitting, throwing or catching. In a games situation, it is the ability to fit these movements to a changing environment which is demanded: an ability to assess the situation, to decide which movement to perform and to time the movement accurately.

It has been shown that individuals differ in their ability to attend selectively and in their reliance on certain modes of perception. From studies so far put forward, some consistencies have been observed in this respect.

As an aspect of personality study, individual differences in dominant modes of perception would appear to be of major importance and deserve more attention than has hitherto been the case.

References

AUDLEY, R.J. (1970). Choosing. *Bull. Brit. Psychol. Soc.,* **23**, 177-191.

BARTLETT, F.C. (1932). "Remembering." Cambridge: University Press.

BAUERMEISTER, M., WAPNER, S. & WERNER, H. (1963). Sex differences in the perception of apparent verticality and apparent body position under conditions of body tilt. *J. Pers.,* **31**.

BERLYNE, D.E., (1969). The development of the concept of attention in psychology. In C.R. Evans & T.B. Mulholland (Eds.) "Attention in Neurophysiology." London: Butterworth.

BOUND, M. (1957). A study of the relationship between Witkin's indices of field dependence and Eysenck's indices of neuroticism. Unpub. doctoral diss. Purdue University.

BROADBENT, D.E. (1958). "Perception and Communication." London: Pergamon.

BROADBENT, D.E. (1971). Introduction. In A. Summerfield (Ed.) Cognitive psychology. *Brit. Med. Bull.,* **27**, 191-194.

BROADHURST, P.L. (1959). The interaction of task difficulty and maturation: the Yerke's-Dodson Law revived. *Acta Psychologica,* **16**, 321-328.

BRUCE, R.H. & LOW, F.N. (1951). The effect of practice with brief-exposure techniques upon central and peripheral visual acuity and a search for a brief test of visual acuity. *J. Exp. Psychol.,* **41**, 275.

CATTELL, R.B. & EBER, H.W. (1964). "Handbook for 16 PFQ." Illinois: I.P.A.T.

DEUTSCH, J.A. & DEUTSCH, D. (1963). Attention: some theoretical considerations. *Psychol. Rev.,* **70**, 80-90.

EASTERBROOK, J.A. (1959). The effect of emotion on cue utilisation and the organisation of behaviour. *Psychol. Rev.,* **66**, 183-201.

EDWARDS, D.C. (1968). "General Psychology." London: Collier-Macmillan.

EVANS, J. (1967). Field dependence and the Maudsley personality inventory. *Percept. Motor Skills,* **24**, 256.

EYSENCK, H.J. (1961). "Dimensions of Personality." London: Routledge & Kegan Paul.

EYSENCK, H.J. (1967). "The Biological Basis of Personality." Springfield: Thomas.

FELLOWS, B.J. (1968). "The Discrimination Process and Development." London: Pergamon.

FORGUS, R.H. (1966). "Perception." New York: McGraw-Hill.

GARDNER, R.W. & LONG, R.I. (1960). The stability of cognitive controls. *J. Ab. Soc. Psychol.,* **61**, 485.

GARDNER, R.W. (1961). Cognitive controls of attention deployment as determinants of visual illusions. *J. Ab. Soc. Psychol.,* **62**, 120.

GARDNER, R.W. & LONG, R.I. (1962). Cognitive controls of attention and inhibition: a study of individual consistencies. *Brit. J. Psychol.,* **53**, 381.

GIBSON, J.J. (Ed.) (1947). Motion picture testing and research. Army Air Forces Aviation. Psychology Research Reports, No. 7.

GIBSON, J.J. (1968). "The Senses Considered as Perceptual Systems." London: Allen & Unwin.

GRUEN, A. (1955). The relation of dancing experience and personality to perception. *Psychol. Monog.,* **69**.

HENDRY, L.B. (1970). A comparative analysis of student characteristics. Unpub. M. Ed. thesis. University Leicester.

HUBEL, D.H. & WEISEL, T.N. (1959). Receptive fields of single neurones in the cat's striate cortex. *J. Physiol.,* **148**, 574-591.

ITTLESON, W.H. & CANTRIL, H. (1954). "Perception: a transactional approach." New York: Random House.

JACKSON, D.N. (1956). A short form of Witkin's E.F.T. *J. Ab. Soc., Psychol.,* **53**, 254-255.

JAMES, W. (1890). "Principles of Psychology." Vol. 1. London: Macmillan.

JOHNSON, D.T., NEVILLE, C.W. & WORKMAN, S.N. (1969). Field independence and the 16 PF: a further note. *Percept. Motor Skills,* **28**, 670.

JONES, M.G. (1970). Perception, personality and movement. Unpub. M.Ed. thesis: University Leicester.

KARP, S.A. (1963). Field dependence and overcoming embeddedness. *J. Consult. Psychol.,* **27**, 294-302.

KLEIN, G.S. (1951). The personal world through perception. In R.R. Blake & G.V. Ramsey, (Ed.) (1951). "Perception an Approach to Personality." New York: Ronald Press.

KLEIN, G.S. & SCHLESINGER (1951). Perceptual attitudes towards instability, 1 Prediction of apparent movement experiences from Rorschach responses. *J. Pers.,* **19**, 289.

LABAN, R. (1960). "The Mastery of Movement." London: Macdonald & Evans.

LOEFF, R.G. (1962). Embedding and distracting field contexts as related to the field dependence dimension. Unpub. thesis: Brooklyn College.

MESSMER, O. (1904). Zur Psychologie des Lesens bei Kindern und Erwachsenen. *Arch. f.d. ges. Psychol.,* **2**, 190.

MORAY, N. (1970). "Attention: selective processes in vision and hearing." London: Hutchinson.

NETSCHAJEFF, A. (1929). Zur Frage uber die qualitative Wahrenemungsform. Psychol. Stud., Ranschburg-Festscgruft, 114.

NEVEROVITCH, Y.Z. Experimental Work quoted by A.V. Zaporozhets, (1958). In N. O'Connor (Ed.) "Recent Soviet Psychology." London: Pergamon.

NORMAN, D.A. (1969). "Memory and Attention: an introduction to human information processing." New York: Wiley.

OHNMACHT, F.W. (1967). Teacher characteristics and their relationship to some cognitive style. *J. Educ. Res.,* **60,** 5.

OLTMAN, P.K. (1968). A portable rod and frame apparatus. *Percept. Motor Skills,* **26,** 503-506.

PAVLOV, I.P. (1927). "Conditioned Reflexes." London: Oxford University Press.

PETRIE, A. (1960). Some psychological aspects of pain and the relief of suffering. *Annals of the N.Y. Academy of Science* LXXXVI, 13-27.

RENSHAW, S. (1945). The visual perception and reproduction of forms by tachistoscopic methods. *J. Psychol.,* **20,** 217.

RUDIN, S.A. (1968). Figure-ground differentiation under different perceptual sets. *Percept. Motor Skills,* **27,** 71-77.

RUDIN, S.A. & STAGNER R. (1958). Figure-ground phenomena in the perception of physical and social stimuli. *J. Psychol.,* **45,** 213-225.

RYAN, E.D. & KOVAVIC, C.R. (1966). Pain tolerance and athletic participation. *Percept. Motor Skills,* **22,** *383-90.*

SCHAFFER, H.R. (1965). Changes in developmental quotient under two conditions of maternal separation. *Brit. J. Soc. Clin. Psychol.,* 4, 39-46.

SCHOPLER, E. (1964). Unpub. dissertation research. In B.J. Fellows (1969). "The Discriminative Process and Development." London: Pergamon.

SHERRINGTON, C.S. (1906). "Integrative Action of the Nervous System." Cambridge: University Press.

SMTIH, F. (1914). An experimental investigation of perception. *Brit. J. Psychol.,* **6,** 321.

SUGERMAN, A.A. & HARONIAN, F. (1964). Body type and sophistication of body concept. *J. Pers.,* **32,** 3.

TREISMAN, A.M. (1969). Strategies and models of selective attention. *Psychol. Rev.,* **76,** 3, 282-299.

TREISMAN, A.M. & GEFFEN, G. (1967). Selection attention: perception or response? *Quart. J. Exptl. Psychol.,* **19,** 1-17.

VERNON, M.D. (1970). "Perception Through Experience." London: Methuen.

WARBURTON, F.W. (1969). The structure of personality factors. Unpub. paper. Department of Education, University of Manchester.

WELFORD, A.T. (1968). "Fundamentals of Skill." London: Methuen.

WHITE, S.H. (1965). Evidence for a hierarchical arrangement of learning processes. In L.P. Lipsitt & C.C. Spiker (Eds.) "Advances in Child Psychology," Vol. 2. London: Academic Press.

WHITING, H.T.A. & JOHNSON, G.F. (1969). The relationship between field dependence, sophistication of body concept, extraversion/introversion and neuroticism. Unpub. paper: University of Leeds.

WITKIN, H.A. (1949). The nature and importance of individual differences in perception. *J. Pers.,* **18,** 145-170.

WITKIN, H.A. (1965). Psychological differentiation and forms of pathology. *J. Ab. Psychol.,* **70**, 317-336.

WITKIN, H.A., DYK, R.B., FATERSON, H.F., GOODENOUGH, D.R. & KARP, S.A. (1962). "Psychological Differentiation." New York: Wiley.

WITKIN, H.A., GOODENOUGH, D.R. & KARP, S.A. (1967). Stability of cognitive style from childhood to young adulthood. *J. Pers. Soc. Psychol.,* **7**, 291-300.

WITKIN, H.A., LEWIS, H.B. & WEIL, E. (1968). Affective reactions and patient-therapist interactions among more differentiated and less differentiated patients early in therapy. *J. Nerv. Ment. Dis.,* **146**, 3.

WOBER, M. (1966). Sensotypes. *J. Soc. Psychol.,* **70**, 181-189.

ZAPOROZHETS, A.V. (1957). The development of voluntary movements. In B. Simon (Ed.) "Psychology in the Soviet Union." London: Routledge & Kegan Paul.

THE BODY-CONCEPT

by H.T.A. Whiting

Witkin (1965) has further extended the meaning of his dimension of perceptual functioning (field dependence/ independence) by relating it to what he terms 'sophistication of body-concept'. Field-independent perceivers are considered to have a relatively *articulated* (see page   ) impression of the body as distinct from its surrounding field and of part of the body as being separated but interrelated in a clear structure.

Although the term body-concept is seldom encountered in the physical education and sporting literature, it is considered to overlap so much with other terminology that an extended elaboration of its usage and meaning would be particularly useful.

Body-concept is a global term embracing a diversity of information pertaining to mental representations of the body gathered from a number of different viewpoints. The relative generality of the term is further extended by the connotations which different writers attach to the word 'body'. Some adopt an integrated psycho-physical approach while others opt for an outmoded mind/body dualism leading to a concentration on the physical attributes at the expense of the mental. Differences of this kind make it very difficult for their readers who are attempting to derive a meaningful idea of the *body-concept.* This difficulty is further complicated by the variations of terminology used, sometimes for similar concepts, and at others for concepts of a more restricted nature. For this kind of reason, it is intended to review some of the work in this area in an attempt to put *body-concept* into perspective since a meaningful and useful unitary definition would not seem possible.

In discussing the concept of a 'concept', Meredith (1966) refers to the process of concept-formation as a special type of learning which, depending upon psycho-physical processes in the brain takes time and requires a variety of stimuli and reinforcements. He continues:—

> The process is never fully determinate for even when the concept is well-established it can suffer neglect or inhibition and it can be revived by

43

further reinforcement or modified by new stimulation. These influences may come from 'outside' through sensory processes which may be exteroceptive, interoceptive or proprioceptive or from other 'formations' in the brain itself. Thus concepts can be influenced by other concepts. It is not far fetched to regard them as living an organic and communal life, requiring nutrition and support and showing growth and interaction.

Such an elaboration is a useful framework in which to consider *body-concept*. The learning involved and the multi-stimulus determinants of such a concept are reflected in Witkin's (1965) definition:—

> The systematic impression an individual has of his body, cognitive and affective, conscious and unconscious formed in the process of growing up.

To Witkin, this impression arises out of the totality of experiences involving his own body and the bodies of others. Systematisation is a function of such development. Information received from many sources is differentiated and integrated into a conceptual framework which is meaningful to the individual. Although differentiating along broad lines between the cognitive and affective, there is obviously a degree of overlap and interaction between the two.

A further indication of the multi-stimulus determination of body-concept is reflected at the interoceptive and proprioceptive levels by Allport's (1955) contention that the body-sense—coenaesthesis (proprioceptive information from viscera, muscles, tendons, joints, vestibular canals)—is not only one of the first categories of information to be encountered by the human organism in its developing awareness, but that:—

> ... it remains a life-long anchor for our self-awareness though it never accounts entirely for the sense of self.

Schilder (1935) extends the concept further:—

> The body schema is the tridimensional image everybody has about himself. We may call it 'body-image'. The term indicates that we are not dealing with a mere sensation or imagination. There is a self-appearance of the body ... there are mental pictures and representations involved in it, but it is not mere representation.

Fisher & Cleveland (1958) point to further determinants in discussing body-image as assessed by Rorschach techniques:

> ... bears little resemblance to the individual's literal body characteristics because the way in which an individual experiences his body from the very beginning is a function of his family and social milieu.

An acknowledgement of external determinants in the form of social stereotypes and social conditioning.

Although Witkin et al (1967) were able to show considerable stability in the development of body-concept in two groups of subjects over a period of years (Group 1: 8-13 years. Group 2: 10-24 years) the *relative* instability is emphasised by Freedman (1961) in his contention that the body-schema requires continual maintenance. This is effected by constant sampling of the environment. Head (1926) made a similar observation many years previously in pointing out that each experience is interpreted in relation to the moment to moment variations in one's postural experiences. This can mean in one sense that exteroceptive information has to be discriminated and interpreted against an already existing background of interoceptive and proprioceptive information. The former category of information would be termed the 'signal' in 'information theory' terms and the latter 'noise' giving rise to the idea of a signal-to-noise ratio which has important connotations in relation to information processing in skilled performance (Welford 1969). Ideas of this kind are perhaps not surprising since it might be supposed that the normal homeostatic mechanisms operating within the body would give rise to a relatively stable background of information to which the organism would habituate (a *normal* breathing rhythm would be one example). When such mechanisms become disturbed—for example during stress or illness—some of the person's attention and information-processing capacity might be diverted to deal with what is now a 'novel' stimulus. Temporary distortions in the 'normal' body-concept would be expected.

McKellar (1965) suggests that body-image changes of this nature commonly occur in the 'hypnogogic' state (prior to falling asleep), under conditions of fatigue, with migraine and even with influenza. The fact that such unexpected changes may be disturbing, leads him to suggest that such a phenomenon should be widely known to adults, to children and to those they may come to anxiously for advice.

Other investigators have reported changes in the body-concept under extreme conditions such as prolonged sensory and perceptual deprivation or under the influence of drugs or alcohol. Francis (1968) summarises some of these findings as follows:—

> There was a report of a feeling of lying on a bed and also that the lower part of the body was immobilised by being held. Another case reported an impression that someone was holding the legs and feet and in consequence the subject could not move them. Yet another S reported a distinct impression that someone was in the pool beside him. The S kicked out at the intruder.

In another context, Fuhrer & Cowan (1967) were able to show changes in body-part size estimation by both males and females under conditions of active movement as against non-movement. The effect of active movement was to reduce under-estimations of these sites.

Terminology

The difficulties over the use of terms are apparent in the quotations already given. Some writers refer to body-concept, others to body-image, body-schema and 'sense of self'. It is not always clear to what extent such terms are synonymous and in particular whether body-image and body-schema are 'daughter' concepts of a more global body concept. Frostig & Horne (1964) for example make the following differentiation:—

> *Body-image*—the 'subjective experience' or 'feeling' that a child has of his own body, derived from internal sensory stimuli and from the impressions he has gained of the reactions of other people.
> *Body-concept*—the knowledge that a child has of his body and of the functions of the different parts.
> *Body-schema*—the unconscious self-adjusting mechanisms of the body which coordinate movements and maintain equilibrium according to the changing positions of the body and the constant inflow of sensory-information.

There is clearly an overlap between the concepts loosely outlined under these sub-headings. For this reason, it would seem useful to consider related terminology before attempting some form of synthesis.

The term body-image is often used in a relatively specific sense but it would appear that Schilder's (1935) use of the term which has already been quoted (page 44) is more akin to a *global* body-concept. Benyon (1968) reflects a similar generality in her description of body-image as:—

> An overall concept of one's body and its movements with relationship to varied environments.

While such a definition is so general and vague as to be of little practical use, it is interesting to note the inclusion of 'movements with relation to varied environments'. For a person with a sophisticated body-concept, the implication is of a form of 'knowing' which is not necessarily conscious and which might be perhaps suitably classified in terms of Polanyi's (1958) concept of 'tacit' knowledge—which is not capable of precise formulation. A distinction is being made here in philosophical terms between knowing 'that' and knowing 'how'. Factual evidence about the body such as height, weight, vital statistics, hair colour etc. would suitably be classified under the first category, while knowing *how* to make a particular response successfully to a particular environmental stimulation without necessarily being able to be explicit on the subject would come under the second category. The point is illustrated by the expert player who when asked 'how do you perform a particular action?' replies 'like this!' and proceeds with a demonstration at a level of performance which is above that appropriate for the inexperienced questioner. In this sense, the person 'knows' which movements to make in relation to particular environmental demands. He 'knows' before he starts the action. He does not need to sample the 'feedback' as the movement proceeds. This implies that such movements are pre-programmed as a whole in the central mechanisms of the brain but does not deny that such programmes have been built up by a learning process in which 'feedback' plays an important part. 'Knowing' in this sense might also be considered as the establishment of stimulus-response compatability which is usefully elaborated by Moray (1969):—

> The assumption is made that an accurate response requires the selection of motor units and their integration from among the very large number of options provided by the motor cortex. One might think that two movements for the initiation of which there is no overlapping of motor units (such as the left and right index fingers) should be more discriminable in this space than, say, the middle and index fingers of the right hand, which share common muscles in the groups which control them. Stimulus response compatability, then, is a matter of mapping points in the input space onto points in the output space.

This kind of 'knowing' would seem to be the concern of movement educationalists. If such a generalised form of 'knowing' could be established, it clearly has important developmental and teaching connotations. This topic will be taken up again later in relation to movement education procedures.

Greenwald (1970) discusses the terms 'image' and 'idea' in relation to responses. In this sense, he is referring to central representations of sensory feedback from previous responses:—

> Response images are reasonably regarded as somewhat abstract entities representing functional response classes rather than specific instances of such classes.

There is in this sense a reciprocal relationship between sensory feedback mechanisms and performance control. A similar viewpoint has been adopted by theorists such as Mowrer (1960), Anokhin (1959) and Adams (1968).

The essential question at this stage, is not the existence of such knowledge, but its generality. It might be asked for example how an effective golf-player 'knows' how much *effort* to apply to a particular putt in relation to the perceived distance of the hole? It is to be assumed, that he is able to discriminate between different 'effort' qualities and quantities, presumably on the basis of experience. The crucial question now becomes, 'is the person who is capable of very fine effort discriminations in golf able to discriminate at an equally fine level say at shove-halfpenny or in a controlled movement on the trampoline?' Further and of equal importance, what kind of experience will lead to the development of either a specific ability such as this in golf or a more general ability which is not task-specific? The majority of the findings in this field are against the idea of wide *general* abilities of this kind (Fleishman 1967) and in favour of the relative specificity of skilled actions. Fleishman does however point out that certain abilities can contribute to a number of different skills and hence are relatively more general. The majority of factorial studies in this area have been carried out with highly selected groups for special purposes. For example, many of Fleishman's most sophisticated studies were attempts to devise selection tests for highly skilled positions in the American forces. This is not to deny the usefulness of the studies, but to merit caution in extrapolating to other populations. It may well be that the use of movement education procedures with younger children (before specific skills play the dominant role) may contribute to a more general 'body-awareness' which makes a contribution towards the development of a wide range of more specific skills. Evidence for such a suggestion is awaited.

Since by definition, cognition refers to the many categories of 'knowing', an ability of the kind outlined would be classified as cognitive. In terms of the perceptual-motor skill model outlined by Welford (1969) and Whiting (1969), this kind of knowledge would mediate between stimulus and response ensuring that the appropriate 'translation' was made.

Benyon (1968) takes up the 'movement' connotation and becomes more specific in operationally defining a *limited* body-image:—

> Each child was 'insecure' with himself, he was not aware of what, where or who he was or exactly how he was functioning with relation to his environment. His body often baffled him as it got him into constant trouble by bumping into things, tripping over itself, getting 'lost' in clothing, and failing to allow him to ride bikes, climb trees, or play ball like any of his friends. He also found himself forgetting about his body often acting on impulse with total disregard for the consequences.

A strictly functional definition in terms of psychomotor performance. It should however be noted that deficiencies of this nature need not necessarily lie in the mediating mechanisms between stimulus and response (Morris & Whiting, 1971).

At another extreme, Wright (1960) refers to the body-image as:—

> ... that aspect of the self-concept which pertains to attitudes and experiences involving the body.

A primary emphasis on the *affective* side of bodily experience. In addition, its sub-classification as part of a larger self-concept suggests further delineation in any proposed taxonomy. Fenichel (1945) is more explicit in his approach:—

> ... the sum of the mental representations of the body and its organs, the so-called body-image constitutes the idea of I and is of basic importance for the formation of the ego.

A stressing of the cognitive—knowing 'that'—aspect of bodily experience and its relationship to wider concepts. In this sense, 'I' is looked upon as virtually synonymous with body-image—an integration of all the information which is essentially personal.

Ritchie-Russell (1958) reflects to some extent the standpoint of Benyon (1968) on movement related to environmental demands in defining the 'body-image system' as:—

> ... that which makes it possible for appropriate bodily movements to be performed in relation to afferent stimuli.

With this viewpoint, an *intact* 'body-image system' is necessary for such appropriate actions to take place. Any deficit as Ritchie-Russell states may affect the ability of the child to fulfil the most basic functions of walking, feeding, dressing and washing.

A concern with the affective side of body-concept is exemplified in the work of Fisher (1966) and Dibiase & Hjelle (1968). Fisher (1966) uses the term 'body scheme'. In elaborating upon the nature of individuals who were associated with certain body stresses, he suggests that:—

> The body-scheme may be conceptualised as a representation in body experience terms of attitudes the individual has adopted. These are experiences coded as patterns of body activation (e.g. involving stomach, muscle) ...

so that:

1. Focus on the back of the body correlates with careful control in expressing impulses and a tendency to convert hostility to negativeness amongst others.
2. Heart awareness is associated with religiousness.
3. Body prominence correlates negatively with interest in food.
4. The degree of attention directed towards the back or front of the body relates to the degree of physical activation of either.

Dibiase & Hjelle (1968) use the term body-image in the sense of the *kind* of body considered desirable to possess. For example, in reviewing the literature in this area they suggest that characteristic body-builds elicit stereotyped reactions from both children and adults when they are asked to rate particular somato-types in terms of personality traits. The mesomorph image is usually perceived as socially and personally favourable and the ectomorph image as having traits which are socially submissive and personally unfavourable. Such an affective connotation has important social consequences which will be developed in a later section.

Body Awareness

The term body-awareness has already been used and it is one that is encountered frequently in the literature, particularly that pertaining to physical education. Some of the difficulty experienced in interpreting this usage lies with the word 'awareness' which defies precise definition.

Fisher (1964b) for example looked at sex differences in body-perception suggesting that:—

> . . . a woman who is highly aware of her body is one who expresses herself with a clear sense of self-identity.

He suggests that for men, body-awareness is related to the gastro-intestinal system. Thus, a man with a highly developed body-awareness may be one who is:—

> Unusually interested in incorporating things and finding adequate sources of supply and gratification.

A more clearer concept is perhaps outlined by Jourard (1967b) in developing his contention of a connection between body experience (defined as: what someone perceives, believes, imagines, feels and fantasies about his body) and physical and mental health. He suggests that a repression of body experience leads to the acceptance of a very high threshold of stress and pain before cognizance is taken. Whereas, someone more 'tuned in to his body' would probably notice the onset of a particular malaise and change what he was doing to (and with) his body in order to gain a sense of vitality and well-being.

In relation to athletic performance, Jourard (1967a) emphasises the merits of a sophisticated body-awareness:—

> Dancers and athletes necessarily have a keener sense of the condition of their bodies. They simply cannot perform when they are not warmed up,

when they are cramped from inactivity, or depressed by an unsatisfactory way of life. They can sense when muscles are stiff, when energy is at a low ebb, when they have eaten too little or too much.

Jourard further suggests that psychotherapists are becoming interested in techniques for awakening a benumbed *body-consciousness*. He points to the high incidence in America of teachers of body-awareness whose work is aimed at undoing the repression of body experience. It is interesting to speculate upon the possibility of movement education as practised in schools forestalling the necessity for such teaching at a later stage of development.

Writers such as Morison (1969) conceptualise body-awareness in terms of general kinaesthetic sensitivity:—

> ... body awareness involves sensing how any part of the body is moving and the effect this has on the body as a whole. Awareness is this sense means knowing by feeling rather than intellectual knowledge though this may be needed in certain stages of the learning process.

Now, while most workers in this area of personality study would be willing to agree that proprioceptive information plays its part in the multi-stimulus determined body-concept, other sources of information (as already outlined) are accorded similar or greater importance by different workers. While it is possible to define body-awareness in terms of a *general* sensitivity to kinaesthetic information it is not at all clear that this is a particularly useful approach. Dickinson (1970) has been particularly critical of such usage, drawing attention to the limitations implicit in a definition of this kind and quoting research evidence for the relatively specific nature of the kinaesthetic sense modalities. His plea for linking concepts of body-awareness to modern theories of attention is shared and was developed in some detail in the previous section (pages 20-26).

The term body-awareness has an historical background stretching back almost as far as that of body-image. As long ago as 1932 for example Alexander (1957) suggested that by his procedures:—

> ... a gradual improvement will be brought about in the pupil's sensory appreciation so that he will become aware of faults in his habitaul manner of using himself, correspondingly as with the increasing awareness of the manner of his use of himself improves, his sensory appreciation will further improve and in time constitute a standard within the self by means of which he will become increasingly aware both of faults and improvement not only in the manner of his use but also in the standard of his functioning generally.

Huxley (1938) was at least implicitly concerned with the concept of body-awareness. To him, a good physical education should:—

... teach awareness on the physical plane—not the obsessive and unwished for awareness that pain imposes upon the mind, but voluntary and intentional awareness. The body must be trained to think ... The awareness that our bodies need is the knowledge of some general principle of right integration and along with it, a knowledge of the proper way to apply that principle in every phase of mental activity.

Summary

Within this brief overview, the body-concept in its totality or in a fragmentary way has been associated by different writers with:—

1 the ability of the body to make movements appropriate to the demands of the environment.
2 bodily sensations
3 imagination—mental imagery which is not purely representational
4 ego-development
5 affective development
6 cognitive development
7 the development of 'awareness' of body functioning and abilities
8 general kinaesthetic sensitivity.

It is suggested that the differential usage of terms like body-schema, body-image, body awareness etc. makes it almost impossible to use such terms if communication with a wide audience is to be achieved. It is proposed to retain the global term *body-concept* and in line with Witkin et al (1962) to consider the cognitive and affective categories of such a concept. It is further proposed that the cognitive category be further subdivided into knowing 'that' and knowing 'how' in the sense already outlined. This is not to deny that ultimately, interest will centre around an integrated body-concept but at the present stage of knowledge, such integration would appear to be difficult to achieve.

The relationship of body-concept to what has been designated the concept of 'self' is reflected in Argyle's (1969) comment:—

Body image may in certain respects overlap the various usages of concepts like ego, self and self-phenomenon relating to attitudes towards the body, it has wider implications which cross-over into other personality areas.

The wider concept of 'self' in this context is apparent from Witkin's (1965) discussion of ontogenetic development:—

It is possible to conceive of the self as an object of experience; and people may be considered to differ in how the self is experienced. One may imagine that during development various kinds of experience—sensations generated by body functions and activities, feelings and thoughts—come to be perceived as emanating particularly from 'inside' and are distinguished from experiences that have their apparent source 'outside'. The activities and attributes the child experiences as belonging to him do not register as separate pieces but form a structured complex, experienced as a bounded 'inner core'. The designation 'self' may be used for the systematised awareness a person has of activities and qualities he experiences as his own. We consider that progress towards differentiation of the self entails a growing awareness of needs, feelings and attributes recognised as one's own and the identification of these as distinct from those of others.

Without at this stage becoming involved in any detail in the concept of 'self' (which is beyond the scope of the present section) it is worth noting Argyle's (1969) differentiation between two aspects of the 'self':—

1 'I'—the conscious subject—the decision-maker.
2 'Me'—reacted to by others as being a particular sort of person, such reactions give rise within the individual to concepts of:
   a) self-image—referring to the perception of the person by himself— what sort of person he thinks he is in a descriptive way.
   b) self-esteem—how favourably he regards himself.

Between them they form a cognitive system which like other cognitive systems exerts a controlling effect on behaviour.

In these terms, an elaboration of Argyle's (1969) taxonomy such as that given below is proposed:

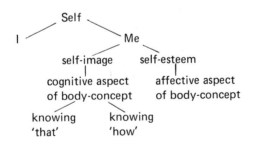

Development of body-concept

The new-born baby probably experiences himself as a 'more or less continuous body-field matrix'. Although current findings on inter-uterine experience and Fantz's (1958), Stechler's (1964) and Hershenson et al's (1965) work on early infantile perceptual abilities would lead to caution in acceptance of James' (1890) idea that very young children experience the world as a 'booming, buzzing confusion', any differentiation at this stage is likely to be very restricted and one view of development would be in terms of progress towards greater *differentiation* (see page 14) within the body-concept and body function. Thus, an original 'global' impression of the body should give rise to an awareness of the parts of the body, the way in which they interrelate in structure and function and their potential for displacement within the environment. That is, towards differentiation of inner structure and function and towards an appreciation of spatial concepts such as 'top and bottom', 'back and front', 'right and left' in relation to the body as a frame of reference. An appreciation will be developed of the body as having definite limits or boundaries and of the parts within as being discrete yet interrelated (differentiation/integration hypothesis) and joined in a definite structure (Witkin et al 1962).

The process is exemplified by Kephart (1960) who suggests that progress towards greater differentiation begins with the learned ability to discriminate between the left and right sides of the body—a progression which is facilitated by the bilaterally symmetrical placement of the limbs, the sense receptors and nerve pathways. Such physical structures provide relatively independent 'sources' of sensory impressions which can be utilised by the child in learning to distinguish between the two sides of the body. Such discrimination is enhanced as the child establishes a preference to use a particular hand or foot.

To Witkin et al (1962), the development of a differentiation between self and field is a gradual process. The development of self is rooted in but not limited to sensations generated by body functions and allied activities. It is rather more derived from all of the experiences which a child encounters during development in relation to his own body and the body of others:—

> Through experiencing pleasure or pain, success or failure, pride or shame in connection with the body and by incorporating the social values which the environment attaches to the body and its parts, the person's body-concept becomes heavily invested with a variety of special and highly personal meanings, feelings and values.

The progress in ontological development from a relatively field-dependent mode of perceiving to a relatively field-independent mode is paralled by progress towards a more sophisticated body-concept. Although persons towards the field-dependent end of the continuum do not differ in sheer awareness of body sensations form those towards the more field-independent end, it appears that they do differ in the nature of the body-concept (Witkin et al 1954). Field independent perceivers have a relatively articulated impression of the body as distinct from the field and of parts of the body as separate but interrelated into a clear structure. Field-dependent persons do not easily segregate the body from its field and regard it in a fused and more global way. Evidence for such a contention comes from the way in which they represent the human body when asked to produce a drawing (Draw-a-person test). In the case of field-independent persons, the body outline is clear and realistically proportional. Body parts are included and given in some detail e.g. fingers, eyebrows etc. Sexual characteristics are indicated and often an attempt is made at role representation. Conversely, the drawings by field-dependent persons show little detail, poor representation of body parts and their proportions, no sexual characteristics and no role representation.

Importance of early influences

In some cross-cultural studies (Witkin 1967) evidence was provided which indicated that differences in the global-articulated style dimension reflect differences in socialisation. While it was considered possible that some differences may be based on genetic influences, it was also suggested that processes in the child's early interpersonal relationships in the family might foster the development of an articulated cognitive style and a more sophisticated body-concept.

Observations made by Dyk & Witkin (1965)—in a study relating family experiences to development of differentiation in children—suggest possible sources for a small but consistent sex difference in performance on perceptual tasks. Women tended to be more field-dependent than men, to have a less sophisticated body-concept and a more global cognitive style. There was an indication that mothers may have different emphases in bringing up sons and daughters: mothers tending to be less accepting of assertiveness in their daughters and placing more emphasis on social skills. It was also noticed that daughters seemed to be reared in ways similar to those found among field-dependent boys. It was concluded that parental influences do affect the development of the body-concept particularly at a very early age.

In this connection it is interesting once again to refer to the cross-cultural work of Wober (1966). Wober has coined the term 'sensotype' to represent the pattern of relative importance of the different senses by which a child learns to perceive the world and in which pattern his abilities develop. It is not altogether surprising to find—as indeed Wober reports—that different cultures put different emphases on particular modes of information processing. He reports important individual differences in a Nigerian population in relation to their cognitive and analytic approach to perceived material:—

It is possible to interpret these results in terms of an elaboration of skills and analytic functioning, not as a generalised phenomenon within each individual but related to particular fields of sensory experience. That is to say the blind lacking a visual world would develop their differentiation and analytic abilities in an auditory world.

Witkin et al (1962) suggest that the differences amongst children in the way in which they represent the body on paper are related significantly to the way in which they perform in the orientation tests in the laboratory. Generalising from this finding, Witkin et al (1967) were able to show the way in which ontologically the body-concept becomes more articulated but stabilised around the age of seventeen years, by the longitudinal and cross-sectional studies they carried out on two groups between the ages of 8 and 13 years and 10 and 24 years.

A marked general increase in differentiation in perceptual function (and hence by inference, sophistication of body-concept) with age up to 17 years was demonstrated and within the groups, children maintained a relative position in their rate of development. Thus, considerable stability in the development of sophistication of body-concept over several years was evident. Witkin et al suggest that, the rise in the cross-sectional curves after the age of 17 years may be partially explained by the selection bias in a field-dependent direction amongst the young adult group.

The overall tendency for males to be more field-independent than females in these results is consistent with the findings of many of the earlier studies already quoted.

In concluding this investigation, Witkin et al suggest an increase in the development of psychological differentiation up to the age of about seventeen years and then a plateau into young adulthood and maturity. There is little evidence as yet regarding the level of differentiation in the very young or the very old. The youngest children in the sample quoted were eight years of age and although work has been carried out with five year-old children, it is difficult to make direct comparison on account of the different tests used for this younger age group. Goodenough & Eagle (1963) and Karp & Konstadt (1963) have confirmed that young children are relatively field-dependent.

While much of the developmental experimental work carried out by Witkin and his colleagues has been primarily concerned with the global body-concept, a number of his contempories (Werner, Wapner & Canali 1957; Liebert, Werner & Wapner 1958; Humphries 1959; Wapner, McFarland & Werner 1962) became interested in the 'body-boundary'—the differentiation of self from environment. Merleau-Ponty (1962) sees the development of such differentiation to be an important aspect of perceptual development and does not really delineate—at least in developmental terms—between 'body-boundary' and 'body-image' except to suggest that realisation of the former is necessary for the latter. In this respect, it is worth being reminded that the skin forms the ultimate body-boundary and it is at this interface between body and external environment that exchange of information takes place.

Jourard (1967b) has been particularly active in pointing out the limited use of touch within Western societies in particular. He suggests that there may be a connection between *body experience* (page 51) and physical and mental health:—

> It's almost as if all possible meanings of a touch are eliminated except the caress with sexually arousing intent. Not that there is anything wrong with the latter; but it does imply that unless a young American adult is engaged in sexual lovemaking he is unlikely to experience his body as it feels when someone is touching, poking, massaging, hugging or holding it.

He points out that increasing numbers of psychotherapists are interesting themselves in techniques for awakening a benumbed body-consciousness. Frostig (1968) makes a similar point in discussing her re-education procedures:—

> A child who is deficient in kinesthetic and tactile sensitivity will be clumsy and awkward and inefficient in his movements and impaired in getting acquainted with and handling the world of objects. Such a child may need both kinesthetic stimulation which originates in movement, and tactile stimulation, through touching and being touched.

Ayres (1963) expresses a similar viewpoint. She provisionally identified deficiencies in tactile functions as a basic factor in 'developmental apraxia' (a disability from which a child has difficulty in directing his hands or his body in performing skilled or unfamiliar motor tasks).

A growing number of teachers of 'body-awareness' conduct classes aimed at undoing the repressions of bodily experience. The latter implies a re-education procedure rather than a stage in development, and is reflected in the early work of Alexander (1957) in the context of a golfer who cannot keep his eye on the ball. He discusses re-education in the following terms:—

> Since it is by means of the use of the self that he (the pupil) reacts to all stimuli, it is clear that together with the improvement in the manner of the use of his mechanisms and in the adjustment of the different parts of his organism, there will also come about an improvement in his manner of reacting to stimuli in every sphere of activity.

On the other hand, the development of body-awareness has been a central theme in physical education (or as some prefer to call it in this context, movement education) procedures over the past decade particularly in the primary school years. Unfortunately, the term body-awareness in a physical education context has been bandied about without clear definition and with little evidence as to the efficacy of movement education programmes in facilitating such developments. Further, the universal claims made by some workers in this area have been noted by Frostig (1968):—

> Unfortunately, the recognition of the importance of movement for development has sometimes led to over emphasis, with movement education being made the basis of all other educational measures. This practice can be dangerous for it sometimes leads to unnecessary neglect or harmful postponement of other important educational goals.

A typical description of body-awareness in such a context is given by Morison (1969):—

> Body-awareness involves sensing how any part of the body is moving and the effect this has on the body as a whole. Awareness in this sense means knowing by feeling rather than intellectual knowledge, though this may be needed in certain stages of the learning process.

A person who is bodily aware in movement is one who is able to use his or her body skilfully in performing basic body-actions of travelling (rolling, stepping and jumping) in the gaining, maintaining and losing of balance and in bending, stretching, twisting and turning. He is aware of the parts of the body required for the action, can select and use them independently of the rest of his body (where appropriate) and knows where in his 'kinesphere' they need to be. The natural boundaries of a person's 'kinesphere' or personal space are determined by the normal reach of his limbs when stretched away from his body. The 'kinesphere' remains constant in relation to his body even when he moves away from the original stance. Thus, the 'kinesphere' travels with the body in general space (Jones 1970).

A similar idea—but with more extreme connotations—is reflected in a more recent report on the 'concept of physical education' (Morgan et al 1970). One of the objectives in physical education as outlined by this study group was designated:—

A movement objective of a general nature.

Since the group could not agree as to the exact nature of such an objective, the report carried alternative statements. It is the second of these which is reproduced here:—

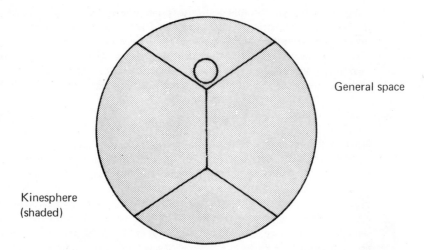

General space

Kinesphere
(shaded)

The term movement sense is used to designate a general condition of motor sensitivity and competence. Like common sense or musical sense it is seen as a consistent personal characteristic operating in a wide field of activity. It implies the ability to move appropriately in a variety of situations both familiar and unfamiliar. More than this it implies a feeling for movement based both upon kinetic experience and the informed observation of the movement of others. Movement thus acquires a meaning for the individual which enriches his daily living and helps him to build a valid concept of himself and his relation with the outside world.

The indefinable quality of beauty in movement is in some measure related to the appropriateness of the movement to the task and the occasion which is the hallmark of good movement sense.

Though it appears as a personal characteristic of a general nature, movement sense is clearly a complex of physical skills reinforced by knowledge and favourable attitudes. The skill complex will include skills with extrinsic objectives and also skills of a postural nature, concerned primarily with the general form of bodily movements. These may extend to the control of gesture and even facial expression. Control of form, though much more important in some situations than others, will tend to characterise the whole of a person's movement.

It is reasonable to assume that movement sense while depending largely upon the individual's psycho-motor endowment will be refined and extended through suitable movement experience. Such experience will include the acquisition of specific skills and also the performance and observation of other, more general, tasks in which a person is led to a conscious awareness and comprehension of his own and other people's movement abilities and to the intelligent and confident use of these abilities in objective, communicative and aesthetic fields of activity.

Huxley (1961) returns to a similar theme:—

> Now it seems to me that we have to think of education also on the non-verbal level. We have to think of the possibility of training directly the mind-body that .has to do the learning and the living. We don't do very much of this at present. We concentrate chiefly on the verbal level and don't do very much for the strange multiple amphibian organism which we possess. There is a very remarkable phrase which Spinoza uses, which seems all the more remarkable when one thinks of the extraordinary abstractness of his writings: he says 'Teach the body to do many things; this will help you to perfect the mind and to come to the intellectual level of thought'. I think it is a phrase of immense importance. If we substitute for the word 'body' the word 'organism' and for the word 'mind' the word 'mind-body', this could be made the motto of an entirely new branch of education, the deliberate training of the mind-body, which then has to make use of its concepts and its words.

The primary sense in which *body-awareness* is being used in these latter statements is that designated 'knowing how' in the model. As previously stated, the major question which arises is the generality of such a concept. Evidence has yet to be produced which would support or negate such an idea. For the time being then, it is an act of faith. In terms of what has already been discussed, it seems to be a desirable objective. It might also be asked in relation to Jourard's statement above, whether the achievement of this kind of objective early in life would obviate the need for compensatory education at some later stage. It remains for educationalists to justify such claims. Movement and play (which at some stages of development may be synonymous) are vital factors in the normal growth and development of the child. Moreover, since movement education precedes verbal education it can be considered to be more basic. The implication of the above statements on body awareness is that physical education in its modern concept implies more than the learning of specific skills and techniques required for games and other activities. Movement is not only functional in the terms expressed, but it is also expressive of attitudes and feelings as in dance. Cooper (1969) suggests that:—

> Physical education can be looked upon as a process through which an

individual learns to appreciate psychologically the capacities of his body; what pleasures he can uniquely express through it and derive from it by means of motor activity.

A concern with the cognitive and affective concomitants of a developing body-concept.

Body-concept and information processing

A return is now made to Dickinson's (1970) suggestion of a linkage between concepts of body-awareness and modern theories of attention.

In terms of the information-processing model presented in the introduction, it will be appreciated that information from the external environment which is not the result of the individual's own actions (exafferent) together with reafferent information (which is the result of his own actions) will contribute towards the development of body-concept. The establishment of such a conceptual framework within the central mechanisms reflecting both cognitive and affective information will serve as a mediating mechanism between stimulus and response. A reciprocal relationship would appear to exist. Information from the internal and external environment leads to a build-up of the body-concept and the presence of such a frame of reference leads to a more selective information intake from the environment.

The linking of body-concept in one form or another with information processing is not a new idea. Fisher (1965) discusses body-image as a 'source of selective cognitive sets' implying that an individual's body experiences produce effects upon his cognitions. Studies such as those of Werner & Wapner (1952); McFarland (1958); Calloway & Dembo (1958) and Hinckley & Rethlingschafer (1951) have related level of muscle tonus, degree of autonomic arousal and body-crippling to the reception and elaboration of particular stimuli. Helson (1958) also points out that bodily sensations contribute to the general adaptation level and hence have an influence on the way in which judgements are made. Concepts of this nature together with an elaboration of the concept of selective attention/perception were made in the last section (page 20) to which the reader is referred back for further elaboration.

Studies on the body-concept

In his paper on 'body-image as a source of selective cognitive sets' (to which reference has already been made above), Fisher (1965) refers to earlier work which presented data indicating that individuals differ in the way in which they perceive their own bodies. Some people, focus more on the right than the left side (Fisher 1958a), some on the back rather than the front (Fisher 1958b); some on the upper half rather than the lower (Fisher 1961), some are more concerned with exterior regions of skin and muscles while others take interest in the interior regions such as the stomach, heart, lungs and other organs (Fisher 1959). These findings, stemming from experimental work, can be compared with an individual's dimensional movement. Considering the three dimensions—up-down, side-side, forwards-backwards, people will fall into groups according to where they prefer to make their movements. This is determined to some extent by their cultural and environmental backgrounds. The Italian for instance will gesticulate with the arms, perhaps with one more than the other. Examples of this kind can be substantiated by everyday observation although stereotypic movement patterns within cultures or sub-cultures do not appear to have received a great deal of attention.

In another study, Fisher (1964a) attempted to determine whether the stimulus characters of one's own body may impinge upon learning and recall, or whether the prominence of one's own body in the perceptual field can affect a type of behaviour which is exemplified in learning and retention. In an attempt to measure such prominence of the individual's own body, he based his results on the answers to the following question:

Write down 20 things you are conscious of right now.

The results were scored by summing the number of references that the subject made to himself. Fisher was here assuming that the greater the individual's perception was focused on his body, the more it would be mentioned.

A further test was to ask the subject to look at a list of words: leg, house, car, thumb, toy, wrist, street, head, tent, skin, hammer, scooter, liver, book, hair, nose, glass, neck, hip, lamp. After one minute, the list was removed and the subject was asked to write down as many words as he could remember. The scoring method in this instance was to sum the 'body' words and subtract the 'non-body' words. A sample of 92 subjects produced results which significantly ($p < 0.001$) supported the hypothesis that the greater an individual's awareness of his own body in relation to his perceptual field, the more likely he was to display selectively superior recall for words referring to the body.

Fisher later looked at sex differences in body perception (Fisher 1964b) suggesting that:—

a woman who is highly aware of her body is one who expresses herself with a clear sense of self identity.

but for men, body-awareness was related to the gastro-intestinal system and thus a man with a highly developed body-awareness may be one who is:—

unusually interested in incorporating things and finding adequate sources of supplies and gratification.

Fisher found that women have a more clearly articulated body-concept than men. These findings were based on three methods of measuring the body image:—

1 Body prominence (as described above).
2 Barrier score—responses to inkblots (Rorschach techniques): which claims Fisher is an objective and reliable test (although others might be more sceptical).
3 Body Focus Questionnaire (B.F.Q.). Here a subejct is shown 91 pairs of words and asked to say which he is more clearly aware of at the time of writing.

Gruen (1955)—in a study previously mentioned (page 29)—wanted to determine whether individual differences in spatial orientation and personality/perception characteristics could be verified in a special group of people such as dancers whose occupation involves relevant experiences. She suggested that one of the objectives in training dancers is that of increasing sensitivity to bodily sensations and this is achieved by providing training in muscular awareness and kinesthetic sensitivity.

Her subjects were given a battery of tests to examine perceptual performance and perception/personality relationships. The tests employed were:—

1 Rod and Frame Test (Witkin et al 1962).
2 Tilting Room Test (Witkin et al 1962).
3 Stabilometer
4 Embedded Figures Test (Witkin et al 1962).
5 Personality—Rorschach
      Figure Drawing
      Interview

She found that the dancers were not significantly different from a control groups of College students on the rod and frame test or the embedded figures test although they were more field independent on the body adjustment test. In a later study reported by Witkin & Oltman (1967), Gruen's dancers were compared with a group considered to be more appropriately matched to his than was the College group. It was found that scores on the body adjustment test were not significantly different either. The stabilometer results indicated that women dancers, like men dancers, perform significantly better when there is no conflict with an unstable visual field. When there is conflict, the performances of dancers and controls are not significantly different. The perception/personality relationships of the two groups were very similar, showing high perception personality correlations on the one hand, and low personality test intercorrelations on the other. Gruen therefore suggests that performance in these perceptual tests is mediated along dimensions extending beyond Witkin's field dependence/independence dimension, but suggests that before valid conclusions can be drawn concerning perceptual/personality relationships, further research is necessary.

Epstein (1957) used a completely different approach to the study of the body-concept. He employed the finger apposition test which assumes that the ability to reproduce finger positions requires a sophisticated conception of the body. The common error here is for the subject to respond on a mirror-image basis which in Piaget's (1952) terms would be considered to be a more primitive response. By incorporating tests of field-dependence derived from Witkin et al (1962) he was able to show a significant positive relationship between field-dependence and performance on the finger apposition test.

Epstein also investigated the accuracy of height estimation by his subjects. The task involved adjusting a luminous rod in a dark room to the subject's own height. It was found that although most of the subjects (who were High School boys) underestimated their heights, there was still a significant difference between performances by field-dependent and field-independent subjects. Epstein suggests that:—

> . . . field dependent adolescents experiencing themselves as shorter than they are appear to undervalue their bodies to a far greater extent than field independent adolescents.

The work of Crutchfield & Starkweather (1953) supports Epstein's work in showing that there is a significant tendency for field-dependent men to identify themselves with the weak and handicapped.

Body-concept and Body-type

Sugerman & Haronian (1964) explored the relationship between body-type as assessed by Sheldon's new (unpublished) technique and Parnell's (1958) anthropometric method and sophistication of body-concept as measured by human figure drawings. One hundred and twenty-six male students volunteered to act as subjects for this experiment, but of these, twenty were eliminated after being somatotyped as their score fell very close to the mean; a further four did not complete the tests. The remaining 102 subjects aged between 17 and 25 years (mean 19.8 years) took part in the complete study. The testing procedure fell into three sections:

1 Figure drawings
  Assessed by Hanna Marlens who devised the original sophistication of body-concept scale. Scored on a 5-point scale (5 most sophisticated).
2 Somatotyping
  Four measures were taken:
   i minimal ponderal index
   ii trunk index (ratio of areas of thorax and abdomen as measured by planimetry or standard photographs)
   iv height at time of being photographed for somatotyping.

Sugerman & Haronian point out that the minimal ponderal index divided the ectomorphs from the other two types while the trunk index divides the mesomorphs from the endomorphs. This procedure was based on Sheldon's most recent revision available at the time and allowed each component to be assessed to the nearest half point on a seven-point scale.

3 Phenotyping
  Measurements were taken of:
   i height
   ii weight
   iii muscle girth (biceps and calf)
   iv femoral and humeral epicondylar diameters
   v skin thicknesses in three areas—over triceps, subscapular and suprailiac, and from these measurements phenotypes, to the nearest quarter point on a seven-point scale, were derived.

From the results, Sugerman & Haronian suggest that endomorphy (Sheldon) or fat (Parnell) is related positively to a primitive body-concept and that mesomorphy (Sheldon) or muscularity (Parnell) is related positively to a highly sophisticated body-concept.

Sugerman & Haronian further suggest that the degree of participation in athletics might be a behavioural variable mediating the obtained relationship between physique and body-concept score:—

> College students who are high in mesomorphy are more likely to take part in strenuous physical activity than others. Through these activities they may gain the esteem of their peers, which in turn may increase their esteem for, and interest in their bodies. Participation in athletic activities might also have a direct effect on their body image. Athletic subjects presumably have more defined concepts of their body boundaries and of their bodies than subjects without athletic experience.

A scale of athletic participation was devised for each student, based on information given in an interview which was used to complete Sheldon's Constitution Clinic form. Each subject was rated from 1-5 and correlations were then computed between these scores of athletic participation and the scores for Sheldon's somatotype components, Parnell's phenotype components and body-concept scores.

Results indicated a close relationship between athletic participation and mesomorphy while ectomorphy (not endomorphy) was associated with a low ahtletic participation score.

This is a useful piece of research if only because there is little evidence of work relating body-concept to physique. Most of the available work has been criticised with regard to its validity. Swenson (1957) and Silverstein & Robinson (1961) have questioned the claims of Berman & Laffal (1953) who suggested that subjects tend to create their own body-type in their drawings and Sugerman suggests that it is unlikely that Berman & Laffal's data are either clinically or statistically significant. The main criticism is towards the tendency of the experimenters to relate the drawn figure to the actual structure of the body instead of the body-image. Silverstein & Robinson themselves conducted an experiment in which 30 boys and 30 girls were asked to estimate their heights and weights, their *ideal* heights and weights and to complete the draw-a-person test. Significant correlations were found between actual and estimated heights and weights indicating a linkage between body-image and body structure. However, Sugerman & Haronian think it more likely that the correlations explain a good memory rather than a link of body-image with body structure.

Fisher & Cleveland (1958) studied somatotype and body-image using Sheldon's somatotype measurements and Rorschach scores from seventy College students as a measure of Barrier index. They found a chance relationship between the Barrier score and body-type concluding that the Barrier score is not determined by actual body characteristics using Sheldon's rating. Fisher & Cleveland imply that the body-image, as assessed by their Rorschach technique:—

> bears little resemblance to the individual's literal body characteristics because the way in which an individual experiences his body from the very beginning is a function of his family and social milieu.

Although they state that body-type may elicit one set of responses from one family and an entirely different set of responses from another, other studies have shown that people do react consistently to distinctive body builds. Both Brodsky (1954) and McCandless (1960) found positive traits were attributed to mesomorphs, less positive to ectomorphs and endomorphs received a definitely negative rating. Similarly, the sociometric choices of these three personality types ranked mesomorphs first, ectomorphs second and endomorphs third. This is the same order which Sugerman found in associating body-type and body-concept: mesomorphy with a highly developed body-concept, endomorphy with an unsophisticated body-concept and ectomorphy in between. Again, Wells & Siegel (1961) asked 120 adults to rate on a 24 bipolar scale pictures of persons with Sheldon's three extremes of body-type. The findings support previous work although the endomorph is not seen as negatively as by Brodsky's students. The mesomorph was rated stronger, more masculine, better looking, more mature and more self-reliant; the ectomorph was rated tense, nervous, ambitious, stubborn, suspicious and quieter while the endomorph was rated fatter, duller, lazier, dependent on others, less strong physically and less good looking. Lerner (1969a, 1969b) reports two related studies in which he found that both samples:—

1   50 males between the ages of 10-20 years
2   90 female students between the ages of 16-40 years

associated the male mesomorph somatotype with socially 'positive' behavioural descriptions and the male endomorph and ecotmorph somatotypes with socially 'negative' qualities. It may well be that very different results would be found in relating female somatotypes with body-concepts.

Dibiase & Hjelle (1968) examined the interrelationships among body-image stereotypes, body-type preferences and body weight. There was unanimous preference amongst all subjects to look like the mesomorph silhouette presented to them (as distinct from the ectomorph or endomorph) which Dibiase suggested might indicate dissatisfaction with their own bodies, and with accompanying personality traits which are assumed to be socially desirable.

A further study relating weight-height ratios, other body measurements and self-perception of the body contours was reported by Cremer & Hukill (1969). One of the most interesting parts of this investigation was the battery of test instruments devised to elicit and measure the student's ability to perceive her body size and proportional dimensions, in fact to measure her body awareness:—

Three complete sets of paired lined drawings of the idealised female figure were prepared, each set containing front and side views in the standing position . . . Students were asked to select the set of paired figures most closely resembling their own and to alter the body lines so that their own body contours were represented . . . A questionnaire was constructed on which students were asked to answer direct questions relating to their body height, weight, contour lines, and body proportions. Responses to the questions were compared with specific body dimension measurements and test scores.

The students were also photographed to obtain a measure of body structure and the projected negatives compared with the student's estimates in line drawing alteration. Other findings from the study support the author's hypothesis that the greater the deviation in weight from that considered 'desirable' in terms of height and age, the greater the difference between perceived body contour lines and real ones.

Kenyon (1968) in a comparative study of attitudes to physical activities suggested that:—

> to some extent attitudes towards physical activity are a function of other acquired behavioural dispositions including body esteem, self esteem, need for approval, social values and relationship with father.

The term body-esteem is not widely used but Kenyon suggests that it can appropriately describe the affective component of the body-concept (defined in Witkin's terms). Thus body-esteem is considered as attitude towards one's body. A measure of body-esteem was obtained from the use of semantic differential scales and based on similar rationale to Rosenberg's (1968) concept of self-esteem.

Johnson & Hutton (1965) conclude that the increase in body-awareness as seen immediately before wrestling matches is transitory. Slusher (1964) reports on greater hypochondriacal concerns among athletes and Thune (1949) points out that weightlifters are more concerned with health, body-build and being manly than a similar age group sample of non weightlifters.

Body-concept and Physical Fitness

Results from the work of Armstrong & Armstrong (1968) suggest that a relationship exists between physical fitness and the body-image for adolescent girls but not for boys. The Armstrongs suggest that:—

> a simple physical fitness score does not discriminate between those boys with a genuine body-image barrier orientation and those without it.

This is because boys are socially pressurised to take an active part in physical activity and many will consequently develop a high level of fitness while being quite disinterested. Girls used in his sample were more free to pursue such activity according to their genuine interests. Secondly, the greater emotional and physical development of high school girls over boys of the same age group may be a compatible factor.

Effect of sensory/perceptual deprivation on the body-concept

Francis (1968) considered some of the factors which might distort the body-concept:—

1 sensory deprivation
2 spatial disorientation
3 temporal disorientation
4 diseases
5 drugs

The method of inducing spatial disorientation suggested by Francis was to anchor the subjects under water in various positions and at various depths. Similarly, for temporal disorientation, the subjects were immersed in water, misled with regard to the passage of time and required to estimate the time they had been isolated. Freedman (1961) and Lewin (1951) also carried out investigations along these lines and suggested that space and time factors do contribute to the body-schema. Familiarity with the situation may however mitigate distortions of the body-image as occurred when divers were used as subjects. Of these factors, it appears that sensory deprivation is the only behavioural way of inducing distortions of the body-image. In this respect it may well be that a child deprived of movement experience i.e. kinesthetic sensory deprivation, will have a consequently distorted body-image which may persist over time. It is also interesting to note that the more extraverted are more susceptible to sensory deprivation than those towards the more introverted end of the continuum (Levine et al 1966).

Body Concept and Personality Dimensions

The relationship between personality dimensions (in Eysenck's 1967 or Cattell's, 1967 terms) and sophistication of body-concept have not apparently been reported in the literature. Whiting & Johnson (1969) in an unpublished study conducted a principal components analysis of the results of tests of field-dependence, sophistication of body concept, extraversion and neuroticism (Eysenck) on fifty ten-year old schoolchildren. Their results showed the relative independence of three of the dimensions and an expected significant relationship between field-dependence and sophistication of body-concept.

Several investigations have attempted to relate Cattell or Eysenck's personality theories with Witkin et al's (1962) framework. Evans (1967) using the Maudsley Personality Inventory and the Embedded Figures Test reported a correlation of 0.39 between field dependence and extraversion. Bound (1957) found no relationship of significance between field dependence/independence and Eysenck's neuroticism dimension. Ohnmacht (1968) suggests that the fourth second order factor 'independence' of the 16 Personality Factor Inventory (Cattell) appears to lack construct validity although Cattell & Eber (1964) state:—

The Independence factor is associated with field independence in the sense used by Witkin, but its full associations are not yet understood.

In his investigations—carried out on a sample of 201 university freshmen—Ohnmacht showed the 16 P.F.I. second order factor of Independence (QIV) not to be significantly correlated with the Hidden Figures Test (a form of the Embedded figures test) stating:—

it seems doubtful that the 16 PF produces a referent of the construct field-dependence.

In a further study, Johnson et al (1969) subjected 61 males and 113 females, (all psychiatric inpatients) to the 16 PFI and to the Rod and Frame Test recording correlations of 0.30 ($P < 0.01$) and 0.07 for females and males respectively. These results suggest a stronger relationship between QIV and field independence than did Ohnmacht's results, but they support Ohnmacht's suggestion that QIV is not a good questionnaire measure of Witkin's concept of field independence.

Body-concept and Laterality

Oltman & Capobianco (1967) suggest that an articulated body-concept may include strongly lateralised bodily functioning; that is, a differentiated system will be clearly lateralised. In an investigation to support or otherwise this contention, Oltman & Capobianco (1967) found that subjects with mixed eye dominance were more field dependent than subjects with established laterality.

Noting Redman's (1968) finding that highly skilled games players among women physical education students (82%) had eye and hand laterality on the same side Jones (1970) hypothesised that Oltman & Capobianco's findings would generalise to such specialist populations. However, no significant relationship was found between differentiation and either clearly defined eye or hand dominance.

References

ADAMS, J.A. (1968). Response feedback and learning. *Psychol. Bull.,* **70**, 486-504.

ALEXANDER, F.M. (1957). "The Use of the Self." London: Re-educational Publications.

ALLPORT, F.H. (1955). "Theories of Perception and the Concept of Structure." New York: Wiley.

ANOKHIN, P.K. (1959). Cybernetics and the integrative activity of the brain. In M. Cole & I. Maltzman (Eds.) "A Handbook of Contemporary Soviet Psychology." New York: Basic Books.

ARGYLE, M. (1969). "Social Interaction." London: Methuen.

ARMSTRONG, H.E. & ARMSTRONG, D.C. (1968). Relation of physical fitness to a dimension of body-image. *Percept. Motor Skills,* **26**, 1173-1174.

AYRES, A.J. (1963). The development of perceptual-motor abilities: a theoretical basis for treatment of dysfunction. *Amer. J. Occup. Therapy,* **17**, 221-225.

BENYON, S.D. (1968). "Intensive Programming for Slow Learners." Ohio: Merrill.

BERMAN, S. & LAFFAL, J. (1953). Body-type and figure drawing. *J. Clin. Psychol,* **9**, 368-370.

BOUND, M. (1957). A study of the relationship between Witkin's indices of field dependence and Eysenck's indices of neuroticism. Unpublished doctoral dissertation, Purdue University.

BRODSKY, C.M. (1954). "A Study of the Norms for Body-Form Behaviour Relationships." Washington: Cath. Univ. of Amer. Press.

CALLOWAY, E. & DEMBO, D. (1958). Narrowed attention: a psychological phenomenon that accompanies a certain physiological change. *Arch. Neurol. Psychiat.,* **79**, 74-90.

CATTELL, R.B. & EBER, H.W. (1964). "Handbook for Sixteen Personality Factor Questionnaire." Champaign: I.P.A.T.

CATTELL, R.B. (1967). "The Scientific Analysis of Personality." Harmondsworth: Pelican.

COOPER, L. (1969). Athletics, activity and personality: a review of the literature. *Res. Quart.,* **40**, 17-22.

CREMER, A.G. & HUKILL, M.A. (1969). Relationships between weight-height ratios, other body measurements and self-perception of body contours. *Res. Quart.,* **40**, 1.

CRUTCHFIELD, R.S. & STARKWEATHER, J.A. (1953). Differences among personnel in perception of the vertical under distorting influence of a tilted frame. Res. Memorandum, I.P.A.R. Univ. California.

DIBIASE, W.J. & HJELLE, L.A. (1968). Body-image stereotypes and body-type preferences among male college students. *Percept. Motor Skills,* **27**, 1143-1146.

DICKINSON, J. (1970). A note on the concept of body-awareness. *Brit. J. Phys. Educ.,* **1**, 34-36.

DYK, R.B. & WITKIN, H.A. (1965). Family experiences related to the development of differentiation in children. *Child Dev.,* **30**, 22-55.

EPSTEIN, L. (1957). The relationship of certain aspects of the body-image to the perception of the upright. Unpub. Doctoral dissertation. New York Univ.

EVANS, J. (1967). Field dependence and the Maudsley Personality Inventory. *Percept. Mot. Skills,* **24,** 256.

EYSENCK, H.J. (1967). "The Biological Basis of Personality." Springfield: Thomas.

FANTZ, R.L. (1958). Pattern vision in young infants. *The Psychol. Record,* **8,** 43-47.

FENICHEL, O. (1945). (Ed.) "The Psychoanalytic Study of the Child." New York: Internat. Univ. Press.

FISHER, S. (1958a). Body-image and asymmetry of body reactivity. *J. Abn. Soc. Psychol,* **57,** 292-298.

FISHER, S. (1958b). Front-back differentiation in body-image and body reactivity. *J. Gen. Psychol,* **64,** 373-379.

FISHER, S. & CLEVELAND, R.L. (1958). "Body-image and Personality." Princeton: Von Nostrand.

FISHER, S. (1959). Prediction of body interior versus body-exterior reactivity. *J. Pers.,* **27,** 56-62.

FISHER, S. (1961). Body-image and upper versus lower-body sector reactivity. *Psychosom. Med.,* **23,** 400-402.

FISHER, S. (1964a). Body-awareness and selective memory for body versus non-body references. *J. Pers.,* **32,** 138-144.

FISHER, S. (1964b). Sex differences in body-perception. *Psychol. Monog.,* **78,** 1-22.

FISHER, S. (1965). The body-image as a source of selective cognitive sets. *J. Pers.,* **33,** 536-552.

FISHER, S. (1966). Body attention patterns and personality defences. *Psychol. Monog.,* **80,** 9.

FLEISHMAN, E.A. (1967). Individual differences and motor learning. In R.M. Gagné (Ed.) "Learning and Individual Differences." Ohio: Merrill.

FRANCIS, R.D. (1968). A conative hypothesis. *Bull. Brit. Psychol. Soc.,* **21,** 241-244.

FREEDMAN, S.J. (1961). Sensory deprivation: facts in search of a theory. *J. Nerv. Ment. Dis.,* **132,** 17-21.

FROSTIG, M. & HORNE, D. (1964). "The Frostig Program for the Development of Visual Perception." Chicago: Follet.

FROSTIG, M. (1968). Sensory-motor development. *Special Educ.,* **57,** 18-20.

FUHRER, M.J. & COWAN, C.O. (1967). Influence of active movement, illumination, and sex on body-part size estimates. *Percept. Mot. Skills.,* **24,** 979-985.

GOODENOUGH, D.R. & EAGLE, C.J.A. (1963). A modification of the embedded figures test for use with young children. *J. Gen. Psychol.,* **103,** 67-74.

GREENWALD, A.G. (1970). Sensory feedback mechanisms on performance control: with special reference to the ideo-motor mechanism. *Psychol. Rev.,* **77**, 73-99.

GRUEN, A. (1955). The relation of dancing experiences and personality to perception. *Psychol. Monog.,* **69**, No. 399.

HEAD, H. (1926). "Aphasia and Kindred Disorders of Speech." London: Cambridge University Press.

HELSON, H. (1958). The theory of adaptation level. In D.C. Beardslee & M. Wertheimer (Eds.) "Readings in Perception." Princeton: Von Nostrand.

HERSHENSON, M., MUSINGER, H. & HESSEN, W. (1965). Preferences for shapes of intermediate variability in the newborn human. *Science,* **144**, 315-317.

HINCKLEY, E.D. & RETHLING-SCHAFER, D. (1951). Value judgements of heights of men by college students. *J. Psychol.,* **31**, 257-262.

HUMPHRIES, O. (1959). Effect of articulation of finger-tip through touch on apparent length of outstretched arms. M.A. dissertation. Clark University, Massachussetts.

HUXLEY, A. (1938). "Ends and Means." London: Chatto & Windus.

HUXLEY, A. (1961). Human potentialities. In S.M. Farber & R.H.L. Wilson (Eds.) "Control of the Mind." New York: McGraw Hill.

JAMES, W. (1890). "Principles of Psychology." London: MacMillan.

JOHNSON, D.T., NEVILLE, C.W. & WORKMAN, S.N. (1969). Field independence and the 16 P.F.: a further note. *Percept. Mot. Skills,* **28**, 670.

JOHNSON, W.R. & HUTTON, D.C. (1965). Effects of a combative sport upon personality dynamics as measured by a projective test. *Res. Quart.,* **26**, 49-53.

JONES, M.G. (1970). Perception, personality and movement characteristics of women students of physical education. Unpublished M.Ed. dissertation, University of Leicester.

JOURARD, S. (1967a). Automation and leisure. *Humanitas,* **3**, 78-85.

JOURARD, S. (1967b). Out of touch: body-taboo. *New Society,* **9**.

KARP, S.A. & KONSTADT, N. (1963). Manual for the children's embedded figures test. Cognitive tests. Brooklyn: Authors (P.O. Box 4, Vanderveer Station 11210).

KENYON, G. (1968). Values held for physical activity by selected urban secondary school students in Canada, Australia, England and the United States. United States Office of Education, Contract S-376. University of Wisconsin.

KEPHART, N.C. (1960). "The Slow Learner in the Classroom." Ohio: Merrill.

LERNER, R.M. (1969a). The development of stereotyped expectancies of body-build behaviour relations. *Child Dev.,* **40**, 137-141.

LERNER, R.M. (1969b). Some female stereotypes of male body-build behaviour relations. *Percept. Mot. Skills,* **28**, 363-366.

LEVINE, F.M., TURSKY, B., & NICHOLAS, D. (1966). Tolerance for pain, extraversion and neuroticism. *Percept. Mot. Skills,* **23**, 847-850.

LEWIN, K. (1951). "Field Theory in Social Science." New York: Harper.

LIEBERT, R.S., WERNER, H. & WAPNER, S. (1958). Studies in the effect of lysergic acid diethylamide; self and object size perception in schizophrenic and normal adults. *A.M.A. Arch., Neur. Psychiat.* **79**, 580-584.

MCCANDLESS, B.R. (1960). Rate of development, body-build and personality. *Psychiat. Res. Rep.,* **13**, 42-57.

MCFARLAND, J.H. (1958). The effect of a symmetrical muscular involvement on visual clarity. Paper presented at East. Psych. Assoc., New York.

MCKELLAR, P. (1965). Thinking, remembering and imagining. In J.G. Howells (Ed.) "Modern Perspectives in Child Psychiatry." Edinburgh: Oliver & Boyd.

MEREDITH, G.P. (1966). "Instruments of Communication." London: Pergamon.

MERLEAU-PONTY, M. (1962). "Phenomenology of Perception." London: Routledge & Kegan Paul.

MORAY, N. (1969). "Attention." London: Hutchinson.

MORGAN, R.E. et al (1970). The concept of physical education. *Brit. J. Phys. Educ.,* **1**, 81-82.

MORISON, R. (1969). "A Movement Approach to Educational Gymnastics." London: Dent.

MORRIS, P.R. & WHITING, H.T.A. (1971). "Motor Impairment and Compensatory Education." London: Bell.

MOWRER, O.H. (1960). "Learning Theory and the Symbolic Process." New York: Wiley.

OHNMACHT, F.W. (1968). Note on the validity of the 16 P.F. questionnaire measure of field independence. *Percept. Mot. Skills,* **27**, 564.

OLTMAN, P.K. & CAPOBIANCO, F. (1967). Field dependence and eye dominance. *Percept. Mot. Skills,* **25**, 645-646.

PARNELL, R.W. (1958). "Behaviour and Physique." London: Arnold.

PIAGET, J. (1952). "The Origins of Intelligence in Children." New York: International Press.

POLANYI, M. (1958). "Personal Knowledge: towards a post critical philosophy." London: Routledge.

REDMAN, E. (1968). An investigation into the nature of laterality amongst women students of physical education. Unpublished paper.

RITCHIE-RUSSELL, W. (1958). Disturbance of the body-image. *Cerebral Palsy. Bull.,* **4**, 7-9.

ROSENBERG, M. (1968). "Society and the Adolescent Self-image." Princeton: University Press.

SCHILDER, P. (1935). "The Image and Appearance of the Human Body." London: Kegan Paul.

SILVERSTEIN, A.B. & ROBINSON, H.A. (1961). The representation of physique in children's figure drawings. *J. Consult. Psychol.,* **25**, 146-148.

SLUSHER, H.S. (1964). Personality and intelligence characteristics of selected high school athletes and non-athletes. *Res. Quart.,* **35**, 539-545.

STECHLER, G. (1964). The effect of medication during labour on newborn attention. *Science,* **144**, 315-317.

SUGERMAN, A.A. & HARONIAN, F. (1964). Body-type and sophistication of body-concept. *J. Pers.,* **32**, 380-394.

SWENSON, C.H. (1957). Empirical evaluations of human figure drawings. *Psychol. Bull.,* **54**, 431-466.

THUNE, J.B. (1949). Personality of weight lifters. *Res. Quart.* **20**, 296-306.

WAPNER, S., MCFARLAND, J.H. & WERNER, H. (1962). The effect of postural factors on the distribution of tactual sensitivity, and the organisation of tactual kinaesthetic space. *J. Exp. Psychol.,* **63**, 148-154.

WELFORD, A.T. (1969). "Fundamentals of Skill." London: Methuen.

WELLS, W.D. & SIEGEL, B. (1961). Stereotyped somatotypes. *Psychol. Record,* **8**, 77-78.

WERNER, H. & WAPNER, S. (1952). Toward a general theory of perception. *Psychol. Rev.,* **59**, 324-338.

WERNER, H. WAPNER, S. & CANALI, P.E. (1957). Effect of boundary on perception of head size. *Percept. Mot. Skills,* **7**, 69-71.

WHITING, H.T.A. & JOHNSON, G.F. (1969). The relationship between field dependence, sophistication of body-concept, extraversion and neuroticism. Unpublished paper. Physical Education Department, University of Leeds.

WHITING, H.T.A. (1969). "Acquiring Ball Skill: a psychological interpretation." London: Bell.

WITKIN, H.A., LEWIS, H.B., HERTZMAN, M., MACHOVER, K., MEISSNER, P.B. & WAPNER, S. (1954). "Personality through Perception." New York: Harper.

WITKIN, H.A., DYK, R.B., FATERSON, D.R. & KARP, S.A. (1962). "Psychological Differentiation." New York: Wiley.

WITKIN, H.A. (1965). Psychological differentiation and forms of pathology. *J. Abn. Psychol.,* **70**, 5.

WITKIN, H.A. (1967). A cognitive-style approach to cross-cultural research. *Int. J. Psychol.,* **2**, 233-250.

WITKIN, H.A. & OLTMAN, P.K. (1967). Cognitive style. *Int. J. Neur.,* **6**, 2.

WITKIN, H.A., GOODENOUGH, D.R. & KARP, S.A. (1967). Stability of cognitive style from childhood to young adulthood. *J. Pers. Soc. Psychol.,* **7**, 291-300.

WOBER, M. (1966). Sensotypes. *J. Soc. Psychol.,* **70**, 181-189.

WRIGHT, B.A. (1960). "Physical Disability: a psychological approach." New York: Harper & Row.

A DUAL APPROACH TO THE STUDY OF PERSONALITY AND PERFORMANCE IN SPORT

by K. HARDMAN

Since Palmer (1933) and Duggan (1937) carried out their investigations into the personality of physical education students there has been a growing interest in this area of study within the profession. This interest became established in Great Britain with the work of Kane (1962) and Hardman (1962) since when there have been many reported studies. Out of such evidence has developed the idea of a stereo-typed personality in both physical education teachers and high level sport participants. Kane for example showed that athletic ability was positively related to *stability* and *extraversion* and this view is quite widely held. The purpose of this section is to show that while such a relationship often exists, there are many pitfalls in attempting to provide support for such a generalization.

One of the major limitations in empirical studies which attempt to relate personality to performance in sport is the drawing of conclusions from purely descriptive data. Such an approach is perhaps to be expected at this stage of Sports Psychology, but it represents only the first of four developmental stages in scientific investigation:

1 A *descriptive approach* in which an attempt is made to identify the phenomena which exist in a particular field of study. In the field of personality and games playing ability this would be exemplified by, for example, an investigation into the personality characteristics of rifle-men and a comparison of this group with groups of players in other sports. The results of such a hypothetical investigation might indicate that this group of riflemen is characterised by a pronounced degree of introversion. The typical sport and personality investigation stops at this point.

2 The second progressive stage is to *give*, or *hypothesise*, reasons for the phenomena observed at the descriptive stage. To continue the analogy of the riflemen, it might be suggested that the greater cortical excitation of the introvert facilitates the accurate execution of the

precise and confined task of rifle-shooting, whereas the extravert, with a lesser degree of cortical excitation, would lack the required control of motor output necessary for such a task. Rarely are such reasons given to support claims that certain personality traits are related to athletic performance.

3 At a third stage it is necessary to show to what extent the hypotheses which have been postulated to *explain* the observed phenomena can be *empirically supported*. This is normally achieved by carrying out experimental work designed to test such hypotheses. If the outcome of the experiments is as hypothesised, empirical support is provided for what had previously been speculation. To continue the earlier example, a laboratory experiment would be conducted in which matched groups of introverts and extraverts would be required to learn a skill which is thought to involve the same degree of precision as the rifle-shooting situation. The predicted outcome would be that the introverted group would reach a given criterion level of performance more quickly. If such a prediction is supported by the experimental results then the hypothesis is made more tenable.

4 The final stage is to use such knowledge in a *predictive* fashion. In rifle shooting for example a decision might be made to select only introverts for international teams in order to enhance the chances of success in competition. (Whether one would wish to proceed to such decision making is both a philosophical and moral problem).

The purpose, therefore, of this section is firstly to examine the available descriptive evidence in the area of personality and performance in sport and secondly to attempt an explanation of the conclusions to be drawn from that evidence. That is to say in Gray's (1968) terms:—

... to (A) discover consistent patterns of individual differences and (B) to account for the form taken by these patterns.

A. The Descriptive Approach:

In this part, an attempt is made to collate evidence and to identify the consistent patterns which are contained in such data. Before undertaking such a task it is necessary to indicate some of the dangers inherent in this exercise:—

1 Research workers have used a wide variety of measurement techniques and it is not always possible directly to equate one with another. Cofer & Johnson (1960) draw attention to this point and Hardman (1968) gives some indication of the range of techniques in reporting studies

using the Cattell's 16 P.F. questionnaire, the California Personality Inventory, the Minnesota Multiphasic Inventory, the Maudsley Personality Inventory and the Bernreuter Personality Inventory. Difficulties arise from the fact that some of these instruments measure source traits while others measure surface traits and, in addition, some researchers have used projective and physiological techniques.

2 The relevant literature spans nearly forty years, during which time methods of personality assessment and particularly methods of test construction, have changed markedly. In this respect, Cattell (1960) comments:—

In the first phase (up to 1950) neither physical nor psychological measures were worth a cent.

3 The results of many investigations have been given a degree of generalisation, by their authors or readers, which are not justified. Keogh (1959) found his conclusions at variance with those of prior studies and attempted to explain the contradiction by claiming that the generalisation drawn from previous studies should have been limited to the specific groups from which the subjects were drawn. This comment focuses attention on the fact that many of the subjects used in personality studies are drawn from academic institutions and, therefore, are not necessarily typical of the general population.

4 A further difficulty lies in the fact that attempts to interpret the findings of investigations have been made in the light—or shadow—of Heusner's (1952) finding, which set an historical precedent in that Cattell et al (1957, 1965, 1970) have quoted these results as being typical of athletes. Constructing a profile from Heusner's findings Cattell (1965) comments:—

The first illustration is the average profile of forty one olympic athletes— but for discussion it might be considered as a single typical athlete.

In view of the fact that Heusner's findings have never been replicated it is a matter for conjecture as to why they continue to influence the concept of the athletic stereo-type.

5 The latter quotation from Cattell (1965) draws attention to another danger inherent in trying to establish an athletic personality type— namely the use of mean scores. Only rarely does a researcher give the *range* of scores obtained in an investigation. Usually the mean score is given which can lead the reader to the conclusion that the group is a homogenous one. Hardman (1968) and Whiting & Hendry (1969) have shown that this is not so, and that some members of athletic groups

seem to succeed despite a wide divergence from the group mean i.e. despite 'wrong' personality traits.

6 Current thinking regarding the personality of athletes (broadly conceived) is also conditioned by the fact that much of the research has been related to the very popular sports. Unwittingly generalisations have been made to sport as a whole, yet Hardman (1968) in a survey of twelve different sports, showed that there were marked inter-sport differences.

With the above considerations in mind, a cautious review of the literature can be made.

Consistent Patterns of Personality Differences Emerging from Reported Research

To enable the reader to examine objectively the findings of much of the reported research the personality scores of forty-two athletic groups are presented in tabular form on pages 84 to 87. All the research reported in these tables has utilised Cattell's 16 P.F. questionnaire and this procedure avoids the difficulty, explained above, of attempting to relate experimental findings based on different personality inventories. At the same time it provides a considerable body of results which can be examined with a view to identifying consistent patterns of relationship between personality traits and participation and performance in sport.

As the 16 P.F. questionnaire forms such an important part of this work, some comments are essential. Cattell claims to have identified 16 different personality traits or factors and to each of these is assigned a code letter. A brief description of these 16 traits would be as follows:—

FACTOR	HIGH SCORE (+)		LOW SCORE (−)
A.	CYCLOTHYMIA (warm, sociable)	versus	SCHIZOTHYMIA (aloof, stiff)
B.	GENERAL INTELLIGENCE (mentally bright)	versus	MENTAL DEFECT (mentally dull)
C.	EMOTIONAL STABILITY (mature, calm)	versus	DISSATISFIED EMOTIONALITY (emotional, immature, unstable)

E.	DOMINANCE (aggressive, competitive)	versus	SUBMISSION ('milk-toast', mild)
F.	SURGENCY (enthusiastic, happy-go-lucky)	versus	DESURGENCY (glum, sober, serious)
G.	CHARACTER OR SUPER EGO STRENGTH (conscientious, persistent)	versus	LACK OF RIGID INTERNAL STANDARD (casual, undependable)
H.	PARMIA (adventurous, thick skinned)	versus	THRECTIA (shy, timid)
I.	PREMSIA (sensitive, effeminate)	versus	HARRIA (tough, realistic)
L.	PROTENSION (PARANOID TENDENCY) (suspecting, jealous)	versus	RELAXED SECURITY (accepting, adaptable)
M.	AUTIA (Bohemian—introverted, absent-minded)	versus	PROXERNIA (practical, concerned with fact)
N.	SHREWDNESS (sophisticated, polished)	versus	NAIVETE (simple, unpretentious)
O.	GUILT PRONENESS (timid, insecure)	versus	CONFIDENT ADEQUACY (confident, self-secure)
Q.1.	RADICALISM (prepared to break tradition)	versus	CONSERVATISM OF TEMPERAMENT
Q.2.	SELF-SUFFICIENCY (self-sufficient, resourceful)	versus	GROUP DEPENDENCY (socially group dependant)
Q.3.	HIGH SELF SENTIMENT FORMATION (controlled, exacting will-power)	versus	POOR SELF SENTIMENT FORMATION (uncontrolled, lax)

Q.4.   HIGH ERGIC TENSION   versus   LOW ERGIC TENSION
              (tense, excitable)   (phlegmatic, composed)

These 16 traits are referred to as 'primary factors' or 'Source traits'. Since these primary factors are not independent it is possible to compute scores on a limited number of second order factors to account for the correlations apparent between groups of primary factors. These second order factors represent major personality dimensions. The principal second order factors are as follows:—

i.	High Anxiety	versus	Low Anxiety
ii.	Extraversion	versus	Introversion
	(Socially outgoing)		(shy, self-sufficient)
iii.	Tough poise	versus	Tender minded
	(enterprising, decisive		emotionality
	resilient)		(Sensitive, gentle)
iv.	Independence	versus	Subduedness
	(aggressive, incisive		(Passive, chastened
	independent)		group-development)

Each personality factor, whether at first or second order-level, is seen as a continuum along which every individual can be located. His actual position on the continuum is represented by a standardised score out of ten, a 'sten' score. The nature and value of these sten scores is described by Cattell (1970):—

> The conventional s-sten ('Standard-score-based sten') scale takes the raw score mean of the population as the central value, (which is, therefore, exactly midway between sten 5 and sten 6), and steps out one sten for each half standard deviation of raw score. Thus, the mean of the scale has the precise value of 5.5 stens. Any raw score falling between this mean (at 5.5) and a point one-half a standard deviation downward translates to a sten point of 5; and one falling correspondingly within the limits of a sten half a sigma upward of the mean point gets 6. Thus, the range of what we would essentially call 'average', 'normal' scores, namely, a one-sigma range, centred on the mean, is represented by stens 5 and 6. Consequently, only when we get to stens of 4 and 7 should we begin to think of a person as definitely 'departing from the average'.

The concept of a hierarchy of personality traits, which is implicit in Cattell's derivation of second order factors from primary ones, is illustrated diagrammatically by Eysenck (1967):—

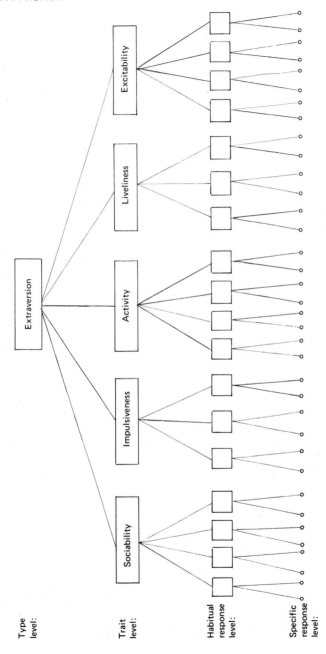

Figure 1 Hierarchical model of personality. (from Eysenck 1967)

Table 1 Mean Scores of criterion athletic groups on Cattell's 16 P.F. questionnaire.

PERSONALITY FACTOR	A	B	C	E	F	G	H	I	L	M	N	O	Q_1	Q_2	Q_3	Q_4	Anxiety	I/E
1. ATHLETICS																		
Heusner (1952)																		
i. 41 Olympic Athletes	5.6	6.0	7.6	7.8	6.4	3.9	7.5	6.5	4.7	5.6	5.0	3.3	4.9	5.1	5.9	6.1	4.2	7.9
Kane (1964)																		
ii. 23 British Olympic Athletes	5.1	8.6	5.9	4.6	6.5	4.0	4.5	6.4	5.1	6.0	4.7	5.8	6.3	5.8	5.8	6.0	5.7	5.1
Hardman (1968)																		
iii. 10 Club Athletes	7.2	7.2	4.1	6.4	7.0	4.7	5.2	6.1	7.1	5.9	5.6	6.1	5.0	5.4	4.2	6.5	6.8	6.8
2. CROSS COUNTRY																		
Hardman (1968)																		
i. 22 Top Class British Cross-Country Runners	5.6	8.2	4.5	6.1	5.8	4.9	4.2	6.5	6.2	5.7	4.1	6.6	6.2	6.3	5.4	6.4	6.7	5.2
Hardman (1968)																		
ii. 13 Club Cross-Country Runners	5.2	7.9	4.9	5.5	5.2	5.4	3.9	6.6	5.9	6.3	3.5	5.9	6.5	7.4	5.4	5.3	5.8	4.4
3. SWIMMING																		
Kane (1964)																		
i. 11 British Olympic Swimmers	5.0	8.3	4.6	5.2	7.0	4.4	4.6	5.6	5.7	4.7	4.7	6.5	4.7	6.6	5.5	6.5	6.5	5.4
Hardman (1968)																		
ii. 10 British Olympic Swimmers	5.8	8.4	5.0	7.3	7.3	3.4	6.2	5.1	6.8	5.5	4.3	5.6	6.0	4.6	5.2	5.8	5.9	8.0
Hardman (1968)																		
iii. 10 Club Swimmers	5.9	7.4	4.5	7.1	6.2	4.6	4.9	4.5	5.9	5.2	4.6	6.5	6.3	5.3	5.0	6.5	6.6	6.0
Hendry (1968)																		
iv. 126 British Swimmers	5.5	7.5	4.4	7.0	5.3	4.3	3.3	5.7	6.3	5.6	7.3	6.0	6.5	6.0	3.7	6.1	6.9	4.8
Rushall (1967)																		
v. 57 American Swimmers	5.5	6.2	5.5	6.5	6.1	5.4	5.7	5.2	5.9	6.3	5.2	5.7	5.9	5.5	4.7	5.8	5.7	6.1

4 GYMNASTICS

Hardman (1968)

	1	2	3	4	5	6	7	8	9	10	11	12	13	14	15	16	17	18
i. 10 Top British Gymnasts	6.0	8.0	5.9	7.3	6.8	5.7	5.9	5.0	6.4	6.0	4.8	5.5	5.6	5.7	6.2	6.0	5.6	6.9
ii. 10 Club Standard Gymnasts	5.9	7.6	4.8	5.2	6.7	4.5	4.8	6.3	5.9	5.7	4.0	6.2	5.4	5.3	5.0	5.5	6.1	5.7

5. CLIMBING

Jackson (1967)

	1	2	3	4	5	6	7	8	9	10	11	12	13	14	15	16	17	18
i. 10 Top Class British Climbers	4.5	8.5	5.2	7.8	6.4	3.6	4.4	6.4	6.5	6.9	3.9	6.5	6.5	7.5	4.5	7.1	7.1	5.5

Hardman (1968)

	1	2	3	4	5	6	7	8	9	10	11	12	13	14	15	16	17	18
ii. 10 Club Standard Climbers	4.7	6.5	3.6	6.2	7.2	3.9	4.8	6.3	7.2	5.6	3.9	6.9	6.1	6.7	4.5	6.5	7.3	5.8

6. TENNIS

Jones (1968)

	1	2	3	4	5	6	7	8	9	10	11	12	13	14	15	16	17	18
15 Champion Players	7.6	5.0	5.1	5.0	8.0	5.0	4.0	4.5	6.0	6.0	4.9	6.5	6.5	5.2	3.4	5.7	7.0	5.3

7. TABLE TENNIS

Whiting & Hendry (1969)

	1	2	3	4	5	6	7	8	9	10	11	12	13	14	15	16	17	18
7 Internationals	6.0	6.0	4.3	5.1	6.4	4.0	4.7	7.4	5.7	5.3	5.6	6.1	6.1	4.7	6.4	6.6	5.3	

8. RIFLE SHOOTING

Hardman (1968)

	1	2	3	4	5	6	7	8	9	10	11	12	13	14	15	16	17	18
i. 10 Internationals	6.0	7.6	4.9	5.1	4.6	6.1	4.3	4.3	6.7	5.2	6.0	5.7	5.3	5.6	6.5	5.7	6.0	4.4
ii. 10 Club Riflemen	4.2	7.6	4.6	7.3	4.3	4.7	4.0	4.1	6.1	5.6	5.2	6.4	5.5	7.7	5.2	7.2	6.6	4.3

9. GOLF

Hardman (1968)

	1	2	3	4	5	6	7	8	9	10	11	12	13	14	15	16	17	18
i. The British Walker Cup Team	6.3	8.0	4.5	5.1	5.7	4.0	4.4	6.0	5.4	6.1	4.2	6.5	5.4	6.2	4.3	6.5	6.6	5.8
ii. 10 Golfers (H'caps 10—18)	5.5	7.8	4.0	6.4	4.4	4.3	4.6	4.5	6.8	5.3	5.4	7.4	4.8	6.6	5.5	6.6	7.1	4.7

Cockerill (1968)

	1	2	3	4	5	6	7	8	9	10	11	12	13	14	15	16	17	18
iii. 30 Golfers (H'caps 0—4)	6.3	—	4.5	7.3	5.8	7.6	3.9	3.9	6.3	6.0	8.0	5.5	6.3	6.2	6.8	5.5	5.6	6.5
iv. 30 Golfers (H'caps 13—16)	6.0	—	5.3	5.6	5.5	8.0	6.2	3.3	5.8	5.3	7.3	4.5	5.8	6.2	6.5	5.2	5.0	6.1

PERSONALITY FACTOR	A	B	C	E	F	G	H	I	L	M	N	O	Q_1	Q_2	Q_3	Q_4	Anxiety	I/E
10. JUDO																		
Hardman (1968)																		
i. 10 Leading Scottish Players	6.1	6.4	3.8	6.1	6.6	3.3	4.1	6.2	7.0	5.8	3.5	7.6	5.3	5.7	3.8	7.3	7.9	5.6
ii. 10 Club Players	5.9	7.0	3.7	6.4	7.2	3.4	4.9	6.0	7.3	5.6	4.1	6.7	5.9	6.3	4.0	7.0	7.5	6.2
11. WRESTLING																		
Kroll (1967)																		
i. Superior Wrestlers	6.3	5.9	5.8	6.5	5.7	6.1	5.3	4.0	4.9	5.6	5.3	5.4	5.7	5.7	6.0	5.4	5.0	6.0
ii. Excellent Wrestlers	5.8	5.8	5.6	6.3	6.3	5.4	5.5	4.2	6.3	5.6	5.1	6.2	5.4	5.2	5.1	6.3	5.8	6.3
iii. Average Wrestlers	5.6	5.8	5.6	5.3	5.4	5.7	4.6	4.3	5.7	5.5	4.4	5.7	4.7	5.7	5.6	5.7	5.8	5.2
12. KARATE																		
Kroll & Carlson (1967)																		
i. Advanced Players	5.6	6.1	5.4	5.8	6.1	6.0	5.6	6.0	6.3	5.8	5.7	5.8	6.4	6.3	5.8	6.5	6.2	6.0
ii. Intermediate Players	5.0	6.1	5.7	5.8	5.3	6.7	5.2	5.2	4.8	5.8	5.5	5.3	6.0	7.0	5.7	5.7	5.3	4.9
iii. Elementary Players	6.0	6.2	5.7	5.9	5.3	6.4	5.4	5.8	5.3	6.2	5.8	5.8	5.8	6.5	6.0	6.0	5.4	5.1
13. ASSOCIATION FOOTBALL																		
Kane (1966)																		
i. Professionals	6.8	6.1	5.1	5.8	5.3	4.2	5.2	5.8	6.1	6.5	5.9	6.5	6.0	5.1	6.0	6.0	6.3	5.6
ii. Young Professionals	5.8	5.7	6.0	4.0	6.3	5.1	5.8	5.4	5.2	5.0	5.9	5.5	4.8	5.8	6.7	4.7	4.5	5.5
iii. Amateur Internationals	5.7	7.8	4.5	5.7	6.7	4.8	3.6	5.4	6.0	4.5	5.0	6.0	5.8	5.8	5.4	6.0	5.4	5.6
Hardman (1968)																		
iv. 13 Club Players	5.7	6.5	4.0	6.2	7.3	4.3	5.8	4.5	5.3	5.6	3.7	6.9	5.5	4.9	3.6	7.3	7.1	6.8

14. RUGBY FOOTBALL

Hardman (1968)

i. The England XV	6.7	7.7	4.6	6.1	6.7	4.0	4.5	6.1	6.4	5.6	4.5	5.6	5.8	5.7	4.2	6.3	6.5	5.9
ii. 17 Club Players	5.4	8.4	3.5	6.5	7.4	3.6	5.5	5.7	6.9	6.2	3.9	6.7	4.9	5.4	4.1	7.1	7.2	6.8

Sinclair (1968)

iii. 32 Internationals	6.4	—	6.0	6.7	5.9	6.7	6.4	3.8	5.7	5.6	6.0	4.3	5.6	5.5	6.5	4.5	4.8	6.5
iv. 48 County & 1st Class	6.8	—	5.5	6.8	7.3	6.6	6.7	3.7	6.3	6.1	7.5	3.6	6.7	5.4	7.5	4.7	4.0	7.33
v. 52 Junior Club Players	4.3	—	5.8	6.9	7.1	5.6	6.4	3.5	7.1	5.8	7.4	4.4	6.5	6.6	6.2	5.3	4.9	6.4

15. AMERICAN FOOTBALL

Kroll & Petersen (1965)

139 Players	6.1	5.8	6.0	5.9	5.6	5.6	5.3	5.5	6.0	5.3	5.2	5.7	5.2	5.6	5.4	6.0	6.0	5.8

16. BASKETBALL

Hardman (1968)

i. The England Squad	5.9	8.1	5.1	6.5	6.5	5.2	5.1	5.5	5.6	6.1	4.3	6.5	6.1	4.9	5.4	6.3	6.3	6.5
ii. 17 Club Players	5.6	7.5	4.2	5.3	6.2	3.9	4.2	5.5	5.4	6.4	3.4	7.6	5.5	5.2	4.7	7.3	7.5	5.1

The 'type' level on the diagram (Fig 1) would correspond to Cattell's second order factors, while the 'trait' level represents source traits. This dovetailing of the theories propounded by Cattell and Eysenck is of great importance for this present work for it allows the descriptive findings based on the 16 P.F. questionnaire to be interpreted in the light of theories of the causation of personality differences propounded by Eysenck. Fortunately, there is sufficient evidence to justify such a procedure. Eysenck (1967) reports an investigation in which he studied the relationship of his own test—the Maudsley Personality Inventory (M.P.I.)—with other established measures. With the exception of the 16 P.F., no other questionnaire correlated significantly with the M.P.I. and Eysenck comments:—

> Cattell's extraversion and anxiety scales had loadings similar to the M.P.I. extraversion and neuroticism scales; they might be used with good justification instead of the M.P.I.

Cattell (1970) supports the above view-point and in his comparison of the 16 P.F. questionnaire with other instruments states:—

> The relation to the Eysenck factors is in principle though not in exact detail, that of primary to secondary factors. Thus, the Eysenck neuroticism and extraversion scales correlate with the anxiety and exvia second orders as scored from the 16 P.F., to a high validity.

The scores for the 42 athletic groups given in Table 1 are mean scores and caution should be exercised in that these scores do not necessarily imply homogeneity in the groups. In addition it should be noted that the tables of norms, from which the sten scores are derived, are based on American male subjects, drawn either from colleges or from the general population. Thus, it should be appreciated that the British groups, reported in the tables, have been standardised on American norms, yet it has been shown by Cattell & Warburton (1961) that there are significant cross-cultural differences.

The results tabulated above may be examined to see if there are any consistent patterns which might indicate relationships between particular personality traits and participation in sport. In addition any such patterns can be compared with postulates previously propounded—for example that games players are dominant or aggressive, stable and extraverted, always bearing in mind that the scores employed in such an exercise are mean scores and give no indication of the spread of individual scores.

High Anxiety versus Low Anxiety:

In view of the considerable emphasis placed on anxiety by researchers in the field of personality and games playing the scores on this important second order factor, as recorded in Table 1, would form the starting point of any analysis. Scores on the second order factor of anxiety are obtained by combining certain first order scores as in the following example:—

FIRST ORDER FACTOR	WEIGHTING	OBTAINED STEN SCORE	WEIGHTED SCORE
C	− .18	5.5	− .990
H	− .17	5.7	− .169
L	+ .19	5.9	+ 1.121
O	+ .30	5.7	+ 1.710
Q3	− .20	4.7	− .940
Q4	+ .38	5.8	+ 2.204
		Constant =	+ 3.740
		Anxiety Score =	5.975

In the above example the scores in the third column are those actually obtained by an individual on those first order factors (column 1), which have been shown to contribute to anxiety. In view of the fact that these primaries each contribute differentially to anxiety, the obtained sten score is weighted to reflect the magnitude of this contribution. The appropriate weightings are shown in column 2 and the actual weighted score appears in column 4. The constant which is added is merely a device to keep the scores on the second order factor within the range one to ten with the mean at 5.5.

Consideration of the above example will reveal that a given score, say a low anxiety score, could result from different combinations of scores at the primary level. Thus two people could have the same anxiety score but yet have different scores on the relevant first order factors.

Examination of the anxiety scores listed in Table 1 shows that thirty-two groups, out of forty-two, have mean scores above 5.5 indicating that their anxiety levels are above average. In most of these thirty-two cases the degree of anxiety shown is not excessive in that the reported scores fall between the mean of 5.5 and a point one standard deviation above the mean. In nine cases, however, the group mean exceeds plus one standard deviation (sten score 7) indicating marked departure from the mean. All of these results oppose the hypothesis that games players are stable. Of the forty-two reported scores only ten support the hypothesis that games players are stable, and all but one are within one standard deviation of the mean. The only result to show marked departure from the mean is that of Heusner's (1952) Olympic athletes; a result which has been quoted considerably and which has possibly lead to the thinking that athletes are stable.

The rather surprising nature of these observations, which shows nine groups to be markedly anxious to only one which is markedly non-anxious, lead to an examination of the contributory first order factors in an attempt to see what influences are operating at the primary level. The example of how an individual score on anxiety is obtained, shows that high scores on factors with negative loadings and low scores on factors with positive loadings will make for low scores at the second order level. Thus a low anxiety score would theoretically result from high scores on factors C, H and Q3, and low scores on factors L, O and Q4.

Cattell (1965) sees high scores on factors C and H as important in athletics and comments on Heusner's (1952) findings in the following way:—

> We note that he (the Olympic athlete) is high on ego-strength, C, on dominance, E, and also on parmia, H, which is a kind of autonomic toughness. In other respects, except for low guilt proneness, O, it is a fairly average profile. The dominance stands him in good stead in heightening competitive motivation and the ego-strength in tolerating the tense waiting hours before a race. Indeed one may conclude that there are many mute, inglorious athletes actually faster than those who win Olympic laurels, but whose lack of worry-resistant personality traits rules them out from performing dependably in such exciting public situations.

In view of the emphasis which Cattell places on high factor C scores in relationship to athletic performance, this would be the first of the anxiety source traits to be examined in the light of reported findings. In studying these factor C scores, Cattell's comment, quoted earlier, that sten scores of 4 and 7 indicate marked departure from the population mean should be borne in mind. Thus a sten score of 7 or more on factor C would indicate marked stability while a score of 4 or less would indicate emotional instability. The tables of results on pages 84 to 87 show that Heusner's (1952) high ego-strength (stability) score of 7.6 has not been replicated in any of the succeeding forty-one studies. In fact, some twenty-eight of the groups have scores below the population mean of 5.5 and are, therefore, scoring in the opposite direction on the continuum to that reported by Heusner and postulated by Cattell as a necessary adjunct of the successful athlete's personality. This movement towards instability is quite pronounced in some six of the reported groups where the mean scores on this factor are more than one standard deviation below the population mean. In terms of the properties of the normal curve of distribution this would put these six groups at a level of emotional instability greater than that of some eighty-four percent of the population. In contrast to these twenty-eight groups with low factor C scores some twelve groups score above the mean of 5.5 but of these only one exceeds a score of 7 to show marked stability. This was the group of Olympic athletes studied by Heusner (1952).

This analysis of the many recorded results on factor C suggests that it would be rash to generalise that games players and athletes are stable; in fact, there is more evidence to suggest the opposite view. However, the point at issue is not whether games players generally are stable or unstable, but why there are these inter-group differences. Information of a causal nature which threw light on this problem would lead to a greater understanding of the descriptive data which is available.

The quotation from Cattell (1965) also lays emphasis on factor H—one of the factors contributing to the second order factor of anxiety. This factor (H) is a measure of resistance to 'startle' or 'fright' and a high score indicates reduced reaction to a given stress signal on the part of the sympathetic nervous system. Such a reduced reaction to startle or stress would suggest para-sympathetic predominance and Cattell describes this as the 'parmic' temperament as opposed to the 'threctic' type i.e. one showing marked reaction to threat. Cattell argues explicitly that athletes should be of the parmic temperament so displaying autonomic toughness.

An analysis of the tabulated results on pages 84 to 87, pertinent to factor H, reveals a pattern similar to that for factor C, in that the findings tend towards the end of the continuum opposite to that hypothesised. Twenty-eight of the groups have means toward the 'threctic' end of the continuum and one is struck by the repetition of scores between 4.0 and 4.4 i.e., scores which are moving well below the population mean. Only twelve groups show a mean score greater than 5.5 and the result closest to Heusner's (1952) 7.5 is 6.7, that reported by Sinclair (1968) for county standard rugby players.

Associated with the concept of a stable, mature individual is the trait of will-power or self-imposed standards. Cattell's factor Q3 attempts to measure this trait and as he shows it loading negatively with Anxiety, one would expect high scores from athletes if one regards athletes as stable, non-axious personality types. Table 1 shows that sixteen groups exceed the population mean, of which one is beyond + 1 S.D., while twenty four are below the population mean of which five exceed − 1 S.D.

The difficulty in interpreting these results for Factor Q3 is that they suggest that games players are lacking in will-power, or self imposed standards. By their extensive training and intense application many games players would indicate that they have this quality to a high degree. The question raised is whether or not this form of application or 'will-power' was employed by Cattell in the life-data which was used in validating the questions used to measure this trait. As these results stand, it would seem that the 'will-power' displayed by athletes is quite specific to the situation and is not reflected in the situations covered in the 16 P.F.

The fourth first order factor contributing to Anxiety is factor L, Protension versus Relaxed Security. The L+ person is suspecting, jealous, withdrawn and irritable as opposed to the L− person who is accepting, adaptable, outgoing and trustful. This factor loads positively with Anxiety, therefore, high scores would contribute to anxiety while low scores would make for stability. Thirty-three of the forty-two groups score above the population mean i.e. in the 'wrong' direction if one looks upon athletes as being non-anxious. Similarly, in the case of Factor O, Guilt proneness versus Confident Adequacy, and also in the case of Factor Q4, High Ergic Tension, or excitability, versus Low Ergic Tension, the distribution of the reported group means is towards the high end of the continuum and would thus make for anxiety rather than stability. The consistent pattern of these results may be seen in Table 2.

Table 2   Distribution of reported group means on the first order factors contributing to Anxiety.

i.   Factors with negative loadings:

	Range of Scores	No. of Groups Above 5.5	At 5.5	No. of Groups Below 5.5	No. of Groups Reaching + 1 S. D.	No. of Groups Reaching −1 S. D.
C	3.5–7.6	12	2	28	1	6
H	3.3–7.5	12	2	28	1	5
Q3	3.4–7.5	16	2	24	1	4

ii.   Factors with positive loadings:

	Range of Scores	No. of Groups Above 5.5	At 5.5	No. of Groups Below 5.5	No. of Groups Reaching + 1 S. D.	No. of Groups Reaching −1 S. D.
L	4.7–7.4	33	0	9	6	0
O	3.3–7.6	32	3	7	3	0
Q4	4.5–7.3	33	2	7	7	0

It is noticeable that in all the cases above, with perhaps the exception of Q3, the distribution of scores is skewed to the end of the continuum most likely to produce Anxiety at the second order level. It is particularly interesting to note that the direction of the skew changes from low scores on the factors with negative loadings to high scores on those with positive loadings. This would indicate that the second-order anxiety scores are a product of consistent scoring on at least five of the six contributary factors, rather than exceptional scoring on just one.

In the light of these results it is surprising that the claim that games players are stable or non-anxious is pursued. An explanation of the apparent conflict between this view and the findings which are analysed above is suggested by Hardman (1968) who shows that top-class athletes are in fact less anxious than less competent players while at the same time displaying a level of anxiety greater than the hypothesised population mean. Table 3 (Hardman 1968) emphasises this point in an analysis of the contributing first-order factors:—

Table 3   Significant differences between means of 167 international games players and 144 club grade players.

Factor	International Mean	Club grade Mean	t Score	Level of Significance
C	4.9	4.13	3.89	1%
H	4.64	4.84	0.95	N.S.
Q3	5.24	5.57	2.91	1%
L	6.15	6.37	1.05	N.S.
O	6.08	6.65	2.71	1%
Q4	6.23	6.65	2.04	1%

Table 3 shows that in five of the six factors the top-class players are nearer the population mean than the less successful players i.e. they are more stable, tougher of temperament, more relaxed, more confident and with greater will-power. In the cases of factors C, Q3, O and Q4, the differences are significant at the 1% level and, not unexpectedly therefore, the figures for Anxiety at the second-order level are 6.36 for internationals and 6.89 for the club player, a difference which is also significant at the 1% level. In the light of these significant differences, it is not surprising that a *comparative* lack of anxiety has been a characteristic of good players and this has led to the belief that such players have a degree of stability greater than the norm of the total population. The figures given in Tables, 1, 2 and 3 would refute this latter assumption, while allowing that there is a difference in anxiety levels between good and less able players. The question that workers in the field ought, therefore, to be asking is why games players display the anxiety levels shown in Table 1 and not merely whether games players are stable or unstable. The causal approach which forms the second part of this work is intended as an initial contribution in this field.

Introversion/Extraversion:

The second order factor scores on introversion/extraversion are obtained by the method described for obtaining anxiety scores. The contributory first order factors are, with appropriate weightings, as follows (see page 89 for calculations):—

First order Factor	Weighting
A	+ .17
E	+ .33
F	+ .41
H	+ .48
Q2	− .16
constant =	− 1.26

Table 4 gives some indication of the distribution of the forty-two group means on this important second order factor.

Table 4.   Distribution of reported group means on the first order factors contributing to Introversion/Extraversion

Factors with positive loadings:

Factor	Range	No. of grp. means above 5.5	At 5.5	No. of grp. means below 5.5	No. of grps. reaching + 1 S. D.	No. of grps. reaching − 1 S. D.
A	4.2–7.6	30	2	10	2	0
E	4.0–7.8	31	1	10	8	1
F	4.3–8.0	32	1	9	10	0
H	3.5–7.5	12	2	28	1	5

Factor with negative loadings:

Q2	4.6–7.7	26	2	14	4	0

Following the reasoning outlined in the previous section, high scores on the four factors with positive loadings (A, E, F and H) and a low score on the factor with a negative loading (Q2) would produce a high second-order score, i.e. marked extraversion. That only three of the five contributory source traits show results in the 'correct' direction accounts for the fact that of the forty-two groups only twenty-six groups show a degree of extraversion while fourteen would be described as introverted.

Table 4 shows that results on Factors A (sociability versus aloofness), E (dominance versus submission) and F (surgency versus desurgency) tend to make for extraversion at second-order level. It is also interesting to note that there is more agreement in the literature concerning dominance and surgency than there is regarding any other factor, with the exception of intelligence. Some seventy-five per cent of the reported group means on Factors E and F are above the general population mean, while some 25% of the results exceed + 1 S.D.

The reason why the results on this second-order factor are not universally high is because reported results on factors H and Q2 tend to make for introversion, that is they are working in the opposite direction to the other contributory traits. The nature of factor H was discussed in the previous section where, because of a negative weighting, the low scores tended to produce a high score at second-order level. As factor H is positively related to introversion/extraversion the low scores on factor H tend to produce low scores at second-order level namely introversion.

This trend is supported by the proponderance of high scores on the negatively loaded trait, Q2. This trait is a measure of the degree to which an individual is either self-sufficient or, conversely, group dependent. The reported results on this trait are interesting because the assumption has been made from studies in the major games that games players are socially group dependent. This could be one of the reasons why athletes are assumed to be extraverted—extraverts are more predisposed to be group-dependent. Table 1 however, reveals pronounced inter-sport differences on the Q2 factor and the scores indicate that there are several groups which are quite self-sufficient, notably the cross-country runners, climbers, rifle-men, and karate players. All these groups exceed + 1 S.D., on this measure of self-sufficiency and this illustrates the danger, referred to earlier, of extrapolating from data concerning major team games to all other forms of sport. It is exceptions such as these which render invalid any generalisations, regarding group dependency or, subsequently, extraversion.

It would seem, therefore, that the claim for a positive correlation between extraversion and performance in sport should be linked only to specific sports. In addition it should be appreciated that some sports attract the introverted personality type and possible reasons for this phenomenon are suggested in the second part of this work.

Tough Poise versus Tender-minded Emotionality

Cattell & Eber (1957) describe a third second-order factor of Tough Poise versus Tender-minded Emotionality. This factor (Factor III) is obtained as follows (see page 89 for the calculations):—

First order Factor	Weighting
A	− .42
C	+ .19
E	+ .17
F	+ .25
I	− .55
M	− .19
N	+ .20
constant =	+ 7.54

In a further publication Cattell & Eber (1962) describe the high scorer on this factor as:—

> . . . likely to be an enterprising, decisive and resilient personality. However, he is likely to miss the subtle relationships of life and to orient his behaviour too much towards the obvious. If he has difficulties, they are likely to involve rapid action with insufficient consideration and thought.

The low scorer on this trait—the tender-minded person—is likely to take too much thought and consideration.

Few researchers have reported scores for Factor III, but Hardman (1968) obtained mean scores of 5.20 and 5.21 for international and club grade players respectively. It would be interesting to know whether the other researchers reported in Table 1 would give similar results, which are, surprisingly, in the tender-minded half of the continuum. This is consistently above the hypothetical mean of 5.5 on three of the contributory first-order factors with positive loadings, namely A, E and F. However, almost equally consistent low scoring on factors C (stability) and N (shrewdness versus naivete) offsets the contribution made by these factors.

Independence versus Subduedness

The last of the second-order factors (Factor IV) is that of subduedness versus independence and the high scorer is described by Cattell & Eber (1957) as aggressive, independent, daring and incisive. Cattell and Eber further suggest that people scoring high on this trait will seek situations where such behaviour is accepted. The low scorer is group dependent, chastened and passive. The contributory first-order factors are (see page 89 for calculations):—

First order Factor	Weighting
A	− .27
E	+ .44
G	− .16
M	+ .32
Q	+ .39
Q2	+ .36
	Constant = − .44

As with Factor III, few results are reported but Hardman (1968) reported scores consistently above the norm of the general population and exceptionally high scores for *climbers.* In the latter case, low factor A scores and high Q2 scores are added to the high E and low G scores which are typical of most groups.

If it is wished to make generalisations about the personality of athletes, Factor IV (independence) would be one area where a generalisation could be made with more validity than in the case of stability and extraversion.

Factor B: General Intelligence:

The level of intelligence displayed by the athletic groups reported in Table 1 is one of the most marked features of the survey. An analysis of the scores on Factor B (general intelligence) shows that thirty-six of the thirty-seven reported scores reach or exceed by + 1 S.D. the population mean. Such observations perhaps constitute the most consistent pattern of individual differences to be noted in this review. Allowance must be made for the paucity of the measuring scale, which consists of only thirteen items and which has led some researchers (Cockerill, 1968 and Sinclair, 1968) to discount the scores on this factor. Cattell & Eber (1957) however, claim a validity co-efficient of 0.80 and a reliability co-efficient of 0.86. In addition one assumes that a full range of scores has been obtained to allow the test constructors to establish a mean population score of 5.5. Therefore, the fact that only one of the reported group means in Table 1 is below 5.5 warrants some consideration, particularly as laboratory findings show little or no correlation between intelligence and performance in motor skill (e.g. Perrin 1921). Hardman (1962), McIntosh (1966) and Boulton (1966) for example, showed that boys from higher academic streams tend to have a greater chance of representation on school and house teams. Such phenomena could result from either a 'halo' complex to which games masters succumb, or to greater identification with all aspects of school life on the part of upper stream boys. Whatever the reason, present results would indicate that the unintelligent do not choose organised sport as a form or recreation at adult level, and this might be the result of the organisation of school and house sport at an earlier age.

Factor G: Character or Super Ego Strength versus Lack of Rigid Standards.

One final consistent pattern emerges from the results given in Table 1 and that is for group means on Factor G to be low. This is a particularly significant finding for physical educationists as, for a long time, character development has been given as one principal value of physical education (Butler 1929; Thulin 1947; Marshall 1949; Dialogue 1970).

Mason (1968) draws attention to the several ways in which the term 'character' has been used in Physical Education and the confusion which has resulted. Factor G, as defined by Cattell, is essentially conscientious and persistent behaviour as opposed to casual and undependable behaviour. It is therefore, related to Allport's (1937) concept of character namely:—

> An enduring psychological disposition to inhibit instinctive impulses in accordance with a regulative principle.

Mason (1968) argues that physical educationalists have ignored character as a concept in moral philosopy and in looking only at behaviour they have ignored the possible role of physical education in the development of moral judgements. The results given in Table 1 would support such reasoning because there is no evidence there that a positive correlation exists between interest in games playing and character as seen in the psychological sense. Rather the scores are consistently low, with some twenty-nine of the forty-two groups scoring below the mean for the population at large and some twelve groups reach or exceed — 1 S.D. If the evidence from a psychological standpoint is negative one must accept Longland's (1955) viewpoint that:

> The ability to play well shows nothing except certain skills of co-ordination of mind and muscle.

Conclusions:

The main conclusions to be reached from this review of studies using the 16 P.F. questionnaire to investigate possible relationships between personality and performance in sport reveals the following patterns of individual differences:

- a) At source trait level participation in sport is associated with:
  - i Intelligence (B+)
  - ii Dominance (E+)
  - iii Surgency (F+)
  - iv Ergic Tension (Q4+)
  - v Protension (L+)
  - vi Instability (C—)
  - vii Threctia (H—)
  - viii Low super-ego strength (G—)
- b) At second-order factor level, participation in sport is associated with:
  - i Anxiety (Factor I+)
  - ii Independence (Factor IV+)
- c) The relationship between athletic participation and introversion/ extraversion shows great inter-sport differences, as is the case with self-sufficiency versus group dependency (Q 2).

   d) With the exception of intelligence the personality trait scores listed
   above show greater deviation from the general population mean of 5.5
   for less-able athletes and games players than for internationals. The
   personality profile for this latter group shows greater personal adjustment than that of the less competent players but it is not superior to
   that hypothesised for the general population.

B. The Explanatory Approach:

   The hierarchy of personality traits suggested by Eysenck (1967) can only exist
if behaviour is systematic. Gray (1968) illustrates this principle by likening the
human organism to a machine with a built in variable component (Fig. 2).

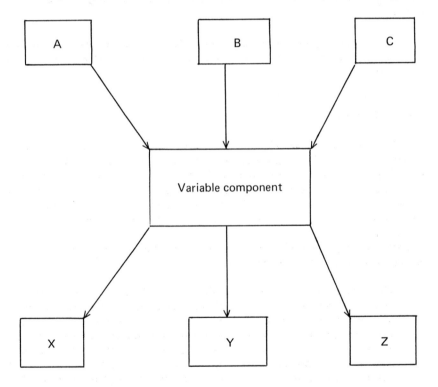

*Figure 2. 'Machines with 'personality'. The 'variable component' allows the inputs A. B and
C through with varying degrees of ease in different individuals, so producing differences in
the frequency or amptitude of output X, Y and Z. The correlation between observation
made on X, Y and Z will form a 'consistent pattern of individual differences'. (from Gray
1968).*

In terms of human behaviour such a 'variable component' which would make for differences in behaviour between individuals, while at the same time maintaining certain constancies within an individual, would require explanation in physiological terms. Gray (1968) makes the point in the following way:

> An organism responds in a particular way to a particular situation because of the state in which it currently finds itself. The state can only be contained as a physical specification of the cells which constitute the organism; above all, as a specification of the two great controlling systems for behaviour, the endocrine system and the nervous system.

Eysenck (1955) saw the implication of the nervous system for personality when he suggested that the central nervous system might be responsible for individual differences:

> . . . particularly the cortex as it is unlikely that peripheral factors could be responsible for the far reaching differences observed between extraverts and introverts.

Anxiety/Stability

Cattell et al (1957, 1970), Cattell (1965) and Eysenck (1967) speak of anxiety and neuroticism respectively, but these concepts may be treated as being very similar because, as already quoted, Eyseck found high correlation between results on the M.P.I., neuroticism scale and the 16 P.F. anxiety scale. Again both psychologists see anxiety/neuroticism as a second order factor and both see the hypothalamus as the seat of individual differences in this important area of behaviour.

Cattell (1965) discusses one of the important source traits contributing to anxiety, Factor H, in the following way:—

> The nature-nurture studies show Factor H to have the highest degree of inheritance found among personality source traits and this is supported by physiological findings, notably that electric heart records (E.C.G.) show a stout-heartedness and smaller and slower reaction to startle in H+ individuals. For this reason, on the hypothesis that the parasympathetic nervous system predominates in these individuals over the sympathetic, it has been called for short 'Parmia' or the parmic temperament. The opposite pole has been called 'Threctia' because its essence is a high susceptibility to threat.

To appreciate this claim of Cattell's, it is necessary to appreciate the nature and function of the hypothalamus. Le Gros Clark (1936) classified the several nuclei of the hypothalamus as follows:

(a) an anterior group having some parasympathetic effect.
(b) a medial group responsible for the important parasympathetic functions e.g. cardiac inhibition.
(c) a posterior group responsible for sympathetic activity e.g. cardiac acceleration, increased respiratory rate etc.

Lovatt-Evans (1949) describes the integration of the above functions as follows:—

> It is evident that, in the main, the actions of the sympathetic systems and parasympathetic systems are opposed to one another. Generally, the sympathetic system brings about changes that enable the organism to react to emergencies in such a way as to maintain a constant environment for its cells, or to help to protect itself by fight or flight, by bringing all its reserves into action, even at some cost. The parasympathetic system is similarly credited with more conservative functions; slowing the heart, reducing light to the eye, aiding digestion and generally serving a recuperative function.

It is in the hypothalamus, therefore, that the highest refinements of autonomic adjustment are effected by the particular and sensitive balance struck between the sympathetic and parasympathetic systems. In addition the hypothalamus has several efferent tracts, two of which are of importance in a study of neuroticism. The first of these two tracts is that which links the hypothalamus with the cerebral cortex. Thus, as it is possible for the hypothalamus to be stimulated by emotion, and as the hypothalamus has a cortical link, so, indirectly, emotion has an arousal effect on the cortex. The second efferent hypothalamic tract connects with the Reticular Activating System (R.A.S.) which will be discussed in connection with introversion/extraversion.

The claim made by Cattell in the above quotation and by Eysenck (1967) is that there are individual differences in the sympathetic/parasympathetic balance.

As the hypothalamus activates the cortex, in response to emotional stimuli, then the individual with sympathetic predominance in the visceral brain or hypothalamus, will respond more strongly to a given stimulus than the predominantly parasympathetic individual. Eysenck (1967) defines cortical arousal from hypothalamic, or emotional stimuli as 'activation'.

It is on the above grounds that Cattell (1965) argues that a high score on Factor H indicates 'a kind of autonomic toughness' and that such a trait would enable the athlete to withstand the pressures of competition. Thus, by implication, the athlete should have high tolerance for stress of emotional nature, i.e. be more stable.

This argument can be represented graphically as follows (Fig. 3):—

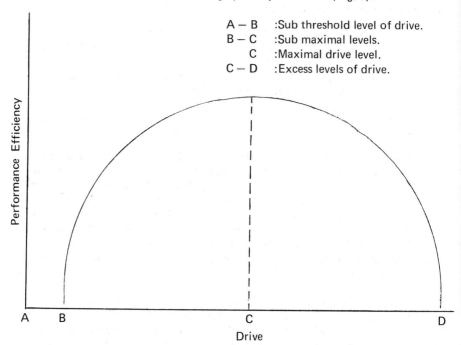

A – B	:Sub threshold level of drive.
B – C	:Sub maximal levels.
C	:Maximal drive level.
C – D	:Excess levels of drive.

Figure 3 Levels of drive and related levels of performance efficiency.

'B' indicates the threshold of drive which is necessary to evoke a reaction, thus, drive levels between 'A' and 'B' are of insufficient strength to effect a measurable response. From 'B' to 'C' the increasing drive level elicits a progressively higher and higher level of performance, with 'C' representing the drive level which will produce the highest level of performance. Beyond 'C' the drive level is so great that it interferes with, and disrupts, performance until at 'D' the deterioration is complete and no overt response occurs, Eysenck (1967) argues:—

> When the correct response is based on a relatively weak habit strength increased drive is deleterious in that the stronger incorrect tendencies gain more in excitatory potential and have, therefore, an enhanced probability of evocation.

Certain conclusions pertinent to performance in games and athletics can be drawn from the above argument:

1   If emotionality is considered as a drive, then demanding athletic events which are strongly emotional for the player, will produce high drive levels.

2   The more demanding the athletic event the more likely it is that the drive level will reach the optimum for performance i.e. point 'C' on the graph, or to exceed it.

3   The anxious person is characterised by low tolerance for stress, and his greater emotionality suggests that 'B', 'C', and 'D' on the graph would be reached sooner in his case when compared with that of the less anxious.

This line of argument would support the claim that games players ought to be stable and non-anxious in that they are less likely to reach levels of emotional drive which are disruptive. However, such reasoning ignores the role played by habit strength in skilled performance, whereby well established skills and techniques will offset the disruptive effects of high drive. This important influence of habit strength in maintaining performance under stress was shown by Standish & Champion (1960) who found that neurotic subjects did well on an easy task when drive was high but badly on a difficult task with similarly high drive levels. It was observed that even with high drive, performance increased as learning progressed.

These considerations draw attention to the fact that it is not sufficient to say that anxious athletes will breakdown in a stressful situation. Rather, that an anxious athlete will produce wrong responses in an emotional situation should *the correct responses have weak habit strength*. Thus, the two factors, skill and emotionality, should be considered together. In addition the possibility of habituation should be considered, so that what was originally a highly stressful situation may become relatively less so. Warburton (1967) made the point that association footballers showed greater anxiety as the competitive standard increased up to the international level. Anxiety scores then dropped off, suggesting accommodation to the competitive stresses.

The problem, therefore, for researchers in the field of personality and motor-skill performance is that if anxiety and established skill levels have to be viewed together than what is needed is work showing the interaction of these two factors. The purely correlational type of study as reported on pages to   , would appear to be inferring from a general anxiety score, based on responses covering many aspects of behaviour, to a situational form of anxiety where other variables (e.g. skill level) help to determine performance.

It might, therefore, be argued that moderate levels of anxiety would be beneficial in the games playing situation in that the hypothesised greater autonomic reactivity of the anxious person could be of value in rapidly adjusting the physiological systems to demands of activity. It is also possible to conceive of situations where the non-anxious person fails to give of his best because the drive level is too low for him but is adequate for the anxious athlete. Additionally, it should be noted that emotional stimuli can effect an increased level of cortical arousal. It has been established that there is a neural link between the hypothalamus and the reticular activating system (R.A.S.). It will be seen in the next section of this work that the function of the R.A.S. is to effect general cortical arousal, thus increasing the efficiency of the cortex. Therefore, an emotional drive would lift both physiological and cortical performance to a higher level in the anxious as opposed to the non-anxious person. This greater reactivity on the part of the anxious person would only be a handicap when drive out-stripped the established skill level.

Finally, any attempt to explain the particular pattern of anxiety scores reported on pages 84 to 87 would be incomplete without consideration of the fact that sport is played for pleasure and that much of this pleasure lies in the arousal of emotions. It could, therefore, be argued that the emotional person is more likely to turn to sport to gratify the need for emotional stimulation than is the unemotional person. The latter is more likely to seek satisfaction in cortical stimulation which can arise from arousal of the R.A.S. which can function without emotional arousal, and which is now discussed in connection with introversion/extraversion.

Introversion/Extraversion

A theoretical explanation of the causation of introversion/extraversion which might make the descriptive findings in the field of personality and athletic performance more meaningful is suggested by Eysenck (1967) in two postulates. The first of these two postulates draws attention to individual differences:—

> Human beings differ with respect to the speed with which excitation and inhibition are produced and the speed with which inhibition is dissipated. These differences are properties of the physical structures involved in making the stimulus-response connections.

The fact that individuals vary in the above respect leads to the concept of different personality types and to Eysenck's typological postulate:—

> Individuals in whom excitatory potential is generated slowly and in whom excitatory potentials so generated are relatively weak are thereby predisposed to develop extraverted patterns of behaviour and to develop hysterical-psychopathic disorders in cases of neurotic breakdown; individuals in whom excitatory potential is generated quickly and in whom excitatory potentials so generated are strong, are thereby predisposed to develop introverted patterns of behaviour and to develop dysthymic disorders in case of neurotic breakdown. Similarly, individuals in whom

reactive inhibition is dissipated slowly, are thereby predisposed to develop
hysterical-psychopathic disorders in case of neurotic breakdown; conversely, individuals in whom reactive inhibition is developed slowly, in
whom weak reactive inhibitions are generated, and in whom reactive
inhibition is dissipated quickly, are thereby predisposed to develop
introverted patterns of behaviour and to develop dysthymic disorders in
case of neurotic breakdown.

In view of the emphasis laid upon cortical excitation and reactive inhibition
in the above postulates some explanation of these terms and their significance
for personality, is called for.

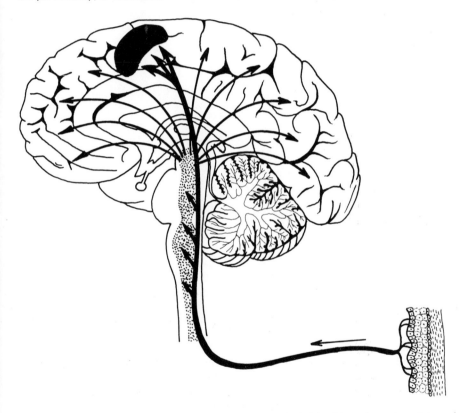

*Figure 4 THE RETICULAR FORMATION is the area stippled in this cross section of the
brain. A sense organ (lower right) is connected to a sensory area in the brain (upper left) by
a pathway extending up the spinal cord. This pathway branches into the reticular formation.
When a stimulus travels along the pathway the reticular formation may "awaken" the
entire brain (black arrows) (from French 1957).*

Cortical Excitation and Arousal:

It is thought that arousal or activation of the cortex or higher brain centres, leads to stimulation of the lower brain centres which is reflected in controlled, restrained or introverted behaviour. The converse would make for extraversion, namely a lower level of cortical stimulation would educe a lower level of control over the lower brain centres which in turn would result in less restrained or extraverted behaviour.

The search for physical structures which would account for individual differences in speed of cortical excitation has lead to the identification of the R.A.S. as the key area. The diagram from French (1957) illustrates the function of this neural system (Fig. 4).

This idea is developed by Gray (1968) who illustrates a series of factors which influence the R.A.S. (Fig. 5).

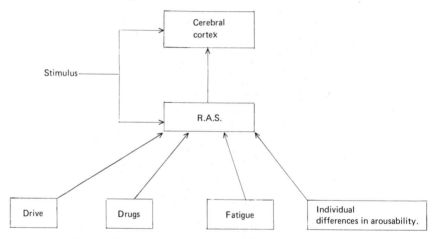

Figure 5 Factors which will influence the R.A.S. (from Gray 1968)

That there might be individual differences in arousability is of great significance for, as French (1957) says:

> The Reticular System . . . is a far more important structure than anyone had dreamed. It underlies our awareness of the world and our ability to think, learn and act . . . The actual seat of the power to think, to perceive, lies in the cortex of the brain. But the cortex cannot perceive or think unless it is 'awake'.

If there were individual differences in the threshold level at which the R.A.S. was stimulated, then the person with the lower threshold would respond to weaker cues than would the person with a higher threshold. Thus the former person would achieve cortical excitation quicker than the latter, or, for a given stimulus which surpassed threshold level for both, the former would experience stronger cortical excitation. The former person would, therefore, be the one to exhibit introverted personality characteristics.

Experimental work has been undertaken to test the above hypothesis, using the basic premise of the Yerkes-Dodson law, as with emotionality, but with 'arousal' substituted for 'emotionality' on the horizontal axis. It is, therefore, important to realise that there is a distinction between these two factors, with 'arousal' indicating cortical excitation resulting from stimuli which are emotionally neutral in character. Such stimuli would not go to the hypothalamus but to the appropriate projection area in the cortex, giving off collaterals to the R.A.S. which in turn would arouse the brain.

Researchers such as Colquhoun & Corcoran (1964) have developed the basic premise of the Yerkes-Dodson law to show that individuals vary in efficiency in response to a stimulus of given intensity. Their results show that the performance curve of extraverts is displaced to the right, thus indicating that the minimal threshold level, optimum performance and disruption of performance all occur later for this personality type compared to the normal population, while introverts reach all these points earlier (Fig. 6).

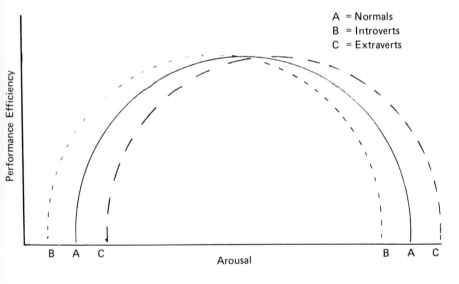

Figure 6 Individual differences in arousal and related performance levels.

These results suggest that:

   i the more introverted person has a lower threshold level than the extraverted person.

  ii the more introverted would perform better under conditions of lowered arousal and worse under conditions of higher arousal.

 iii the more extraverted person would perform worse under conditions of lowered arousal and better under conditions of higher arousal.

 iv the displacement of the curve to the left for the more introverted person and to the right for the more extraverted person reflects the relative strength of the nervous system in the two groups, namely a weak nervous system for the introverts and a strong nervous system for the extraverts.

Colquhoun & Corcoran (1964) postulated that if the more introverted persons are higher on arousal than the extraverts then the two groups should react differently in given arousal conditions. Using sleep as a de-arousing condition, and incentives and loud noise as arousing conditions, they checked performance on simple and difficult tasks and concluded that the performance of the less aroused subjects (extraverts) deteriorated when arousal level was reduced. In addition the more aroused subjects (introverts) were not only less affected but would improve if the original arousal was beyond the optimum (Fig. 7).

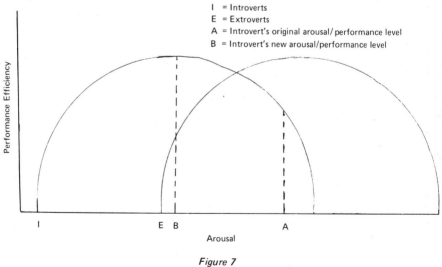

Figure 7

The reverse would apply if the arousal level was increased.

A further extension of this theory is that as sensory thresholds depend on excitation and as this is greater in the more introverted person because of higher efficiency of performance associated with cortical excitation, then their sensory threshold should be lower. This has been checked in the experimental field. Smith (1966) has shown that in response to auditory stimuli the more introverted group had significantly lower thresholds than the more extraverted group, while Dunstone (1964) found a lower threshold of electrical vestibular stimulation in an introverted group.

Significant work in this area for physical education concerns personality and pain tolerance. Following on from the work above, that introverts have a higher degree of arousal, therefore, more excitation for a given stimulus, therefore lower sensory thresholds, then such subjects ought to experience more pain from a given pain producing stimulus. Conversely extraverts should be more tolerant of pain.

Lynn & Eysenck (1961) tested the above hypothesis using heat as a pain stimulus and found that:

Extraverstion correlated + .69 with pain measures while
Introversion correlated − .36 with the same measures.

Poser (1960) using pressure as a pain stimulus obtained a correlation with extraversion of 0.53.

Howarth (1963) obtained samples of extraverts, normals and introverts (20, 19 and 19 subjects respectively) from 309 students. Holding neuroticism constant he applied a series of laboratory measures, one of which was leg persistence, i.e. holding the leg out for as long as possible. This patently becomes a pain producing situation and the scores for three groups were: Extraverts 76.2 secs, Intermediates 79.4 secs, Introverts 59.7 secs. The difference between the extraverted and introverted groups was in the hypothesised direction and exceeded the 5% level of significance. The Intermediate score was unexpected in that it was higher than the extravert score, but not significantly so.

Ryan & Kovacic (1966) looked at contact athletes, non-contact athletes and non-athletes in terms of differences in pain thresholds and pain tolerance. Using heat for the pain threshold and pressure on the tibia and muscle ischemia (work with a restricted blood supply) as measures of pain tolerance their results were as follows:

i no significant differences in pain threshold.
ii highly significant differences in pain tolerance with the contact athletes tolerating most pain, followed by non-contact athletes, with non-athletes tolerating least.
iii Interesting differences existed between the groups on a test-retest basis.

The contact athletes improved by a mean of 28.61.
The non-contact athletes improved by a mean of 9.21
The non-atheltes decreased by a mean of 11.06

Such findings are related by the authors, to Petrie's (1967) perceptual types viz. reducers and augmenters. The 'Reducers' reduce the perceptual intensity of the stimulation while the augmenters increase it. 'Reducers' have been shown by Eysenck (1967) to be more extraverted and less tolerant of sensory deprivation. This would be in keeping with his theory that extraverts are more tolerant of pain while introverts are more tolerant of sensory deprivation. Ryan & Kovacic conclude from their study:—

> It may be that if *reducers* suffer from lack of stimulation they would need change, movement, speed and possibly body contact. Athletics would be the child's answer to sensory deprivation.

Again this would support Eysenck's postulate that there is a certain degree of stimulus hunger in extraverts and a degree of stimulus aversion in introverts.

Costello & Eysenck (1961) showed that the high extravert subjects were much more persistent in physical tasks in which pain entered. This persistence could be reduced by stimulant drugs which presumably lower (pain) thresholds.

By far the major part of the reported research supports the hypothesis of lowered sensory thresholds in introverts, with occasional researchers failing to replicate results e.g. Levine & Tursky (1966) and Ryan & Kovacic (1966) re pain threshold.

As the work on lowered sensory thresholds, quoted above, has raised the concept of sensory deprivation, and better tolerance of sensory deprivation conditions by introverts, it would be appropriate to examine the theory underlying this viewpoint and the relevant research. Recalling the function of the R.A.S. and the fact that it can be aroused more easily in introverts than in extraverts, it follows that the introvert is much more likely to be overstimulated, or bombarded with afferent stimuli, than the extravert. The characteristic of the introvert, therefore, would be his tendency to avoid stimulation which he could do by filtering the inputs and by habituation. Should the introvert find himself in conditions of reduced stimulation, as in a perceptual or sensory deprivation experiment, he ought to show less personal disturbance than the extravert who normally seeks, or relies upon, a higher level of stimulation.

Tranel (1962) studied the effect of perceptual isolation on introverts and extraverts and found that the introverts bore these conditions better. He theorises that:—

> The introvert's greater inclination to be passive and to adhere to instruction is in contrast to the extravert's greater action orientation and inclination to modify external conditions to alleviate discomfort.

Rossi & Salmon (1965) subjected 11 extraverts and 7 introverts to two three-hour sessions of sensory deprivation (1 in comfortable conditions, 1 in uncomfortable conditions). The subjects completed an adjectival check off list in both sessions and a 'discomfort index' established on the mean proportionate drop in self-rated well-being, following the second session. The results supported Tranel's view that the extraverts were more discomforted than the introverts by sensory deprivation.

Reed & McKenna (1964) argued that in sensory deprivation conditions the introvert would divert himself by turning his psychic energies in on himself while the extravert would be deprived of his external cues. As both will judge the passage of time by the number of mental events the introvert should be better able to judge the passing of time than the extravert. The results of their experiment confirmed this hypothesis.

Reactive Inhibition

So far, only the speed of cortical excitation has been discussed with regard to typological differences. Now, the concept of reactive inhibition must be examined to account for certain behavioural differences between the more introverted and the more extraverted person. The considerable body of work concerning reactive inhibition is based on Hull's (1943) premise that:—

Whenever any reaction is evoked in an organism there is left a state which acts as a primary negative motivation in that it has an innate capacity to produce a cessation of the activity which produced that state.

Hull believed that reaction potential, or performance, was the product of drive and habit strength and that reactive inhibition was a form of negative drive. When this negative drive equals the positive drive then the two cancel out and the organism takes what might be considered as a compulsory rest period. During such a rest period reactive inhibition would dissipate, the positive drive would gain in ascendancy and the original reaction would again be evoked.

The above theories have been investigated in a number of ways. It has been shown that the performance curves of introverts and extraverts are different under massed and distributed practice conditions. During the massing of practice (in laboratory terms this would be, say, 30 secs. work—10 secs. rest) the performance of extraverts would be inferior to that of introverts due to the negative effect of reactive inhibition. However, the reminiscence effects i.e. 'increment in learning which occurs during a rest', (Hovland 1951) would be greater for extraverts showing that the massed practice conditions did not favour the extraverts, in that their 'performance' curves did not truly reflect their 'learning'.

Bills (1931) used the term 'blocking' to represent response produced inhibition and I.R.P. (Involuntary rest pause) to represent the 'compulsory rest' described above, during which the negative drive would be dissipated.

Spielman (1963) using the M.P.I. selected 5 extraverts and 5 introverts from a group of 90 subjects. The ten subjects were then given the task of tapping on a plate with a metal stylus. The time between taps was taken and the extraverted group had significantly more I.R.P.s than the introverted group and an earlier onset of these I.R.P.s The results showed that:

The 5 I subjects produced 25 I.R.P.s. (none more than 0.5 secs)
The 5 E subjects produced 370 I.R.P.s. (44 over 0.5 secs)

Bakan et al (1963) applied the theory to vigilance tasks arguing that extraverts should be inferior in that they would miss more cues—such mistakes resulting from an I.R.P. coinciding with a cue. This they subsequently found, and have been supported since by Halcomb & Kirk (1965) and Hogan (1966) using other personality inventories. Interestingly Bakan et al (1963) found that the extraverts did better in group situations while the introverts did better in isolation. This would link with earlier work by Bakan (1959) who found that extraverts improved with the addition of a secondary task. It would appear that such distraction aids the extravert by delaying or offsetting reactive inhibition; or alternatively, in Bakan et al's (1963) experiment the social conditions acted as additional 'drive' for the extravert and distraction for the introvert.

Briefly, the wide significance of I.R.P.s and personality can be seen from the following list given by Eysenck (1967):—

Reed (1961) audiometric response consistency better in introverted groups of children.

Howarth (1963) greater consistency of introverts in line drawing.

Rankin (1963) extraverts have lower reading-test reliabilities, and they also vary from beginning to the end of any one test.

Eysenck (1959) better problem solving efficiency of introverts.

Child (1964) better school performance of introverts.

Furneaux (1962) better university performance of introverts.

Child (1964) and Otto (1965) both found a negative correlation between achievement and reminiscence; (reminiscence being greater in extraverts).

The conclusion to be drawn from the above findings is that consistency of work is better for introverts than extraverts because of the relative infrequency of involuntary rest pauses.

At this point it would be useful to introduce two different approaches to the study of introversion/extraversion, one stemming from Pavlov (1927) centred on conditioning, and that of Witkin et al's (1962) 'psychological differentiation'.

a. Teplov's Approach: Physiological to Psychological

Gray (1968) relates the Pavlovian tradition and that of Eysenck in the following way:

> Notice that they (the Teplov group) started with a conceptual nervous system (Pavlov's) and then set out to look for the patterns of individual differences which they would expect to find if there is variation between the individuals in the functioning of the CNS. Eysenck, on the other hand, started out with a detailed description of the ways in which human individual differences do fall into consistent patterns, and then sought for a causal explanation of them.

Gray suggests that these two approaches are about to meet on common ground, namely that of the R.A.S.

The following points are an attempt to summarise Gray's excellent account of the Russian work:

   i the individual with a weak nervous system is an individual of high arousability.

   ii such individuals will show a deterioration under conditions of high arousability.

  iii such individuals will be more efficient under conditions of low arousability.

  iv following on from i. ii. above, the absolute sensory threshold ought to be lower for individuals with a weak nervous system.

   v Nebylitsyn has shown this to be true for the visual and auditory modalities.

  vi Nebylitsyn has also shown that a reduction in the intensity of a stimulus affected adversely the speed of reaction of the strong CNS individual.

The parallel between these conclusions and those drawn earlier are obvious and it is indeed tempting to equate introversion with the 'weak nervous system'.

b. Witkin's Approach: Psychological Differentiation

The link between Introverstion/Extraversion in Eysenck's terms and Field Independence/Field Dependence in Witkin's terms is not as clear cut as between Eysenck and Teplov described above.

Field Dependence is defined by Witkin et al (1962) as:

> A continuum ranging from analytic perception in which the individual sees segments of his environment as distinct from their background, the global perception in which the influence of the background is difficult to overcome.

Bloomberg (1965) adds:

> Field Independence seems to involve the ability to attend selectively to relevant aspects of stimulation while avoiding or withholding attention from irrelevant aspects.

Barret, McCabe & Thornton (1967) proved that the differences in perceptual style described above were not a function of visual measures, and, thereby supported Witkin's view that perceptual style was a function of individual psychological differentiation.

Evans (1967) attempted to link visual style with introversion/extraversion. He obtained a positive correlation of 0.39 between Field Dependence and Extraversion which was significant at the 5% level. Correlation with Eysenck's Neuroticism was non-significant.

While this is a somewhat tenuous connection between the two concepts and accepting that there are conflicting findings, there is a body of work relating visual style to measure of pain, distraction arousal etc. paralleling the connection between those variables and introversion/extraversion. This work is summarised as follows:

Bloomberg (1965) gave a reversible perspective task to groups of Field independent (F.I.) and Field dependant (F.D.) subjects and then added the (distracting) task of repeating digits. The F.I. subjects showed the greater decrement as did the introverted group in the experiments of Claridge (1960) and Bakan (1959) previously quoted.

Oltman (1964) uses Callaway's Concept of 'narrowed attention' and suggests that physiological arousal leads to a reduction in responsiveness to peripheral cues. Again a parallel with the greater arousal of the introvert and field independence can be drawn.

Sweeney and Fine (1965) looked at pain reactivity and Field Dependence in a sample of 71 young soldiers, using cold water as a pain stimulus. They conclude:—

Under equivalent conditions the individual who experiences great pain is an analytic perceiver who tends to extract and focus upon the most overwhelming aspect of his environment. The global perceiver, on the other hand, tends to experience pain as embedded in the environmental structure; the tendency is reflected in lower judgements of pain intensity.

Solar & Davenport (1964) investigated social compliance as a function of field dependence. Ten F.D. subjects and 10 F.I. subjects were tested on the Rod and Frame test. The subjects were then paired to give one F.D. and one F.I. subject to each pair. The two subjects working together were retested and in each case the mean displacement for the pair was in the direction of the field independent persons original score. This suggested that the field dependent persons were influenced by social pressures. Again this relates to Eysenck's view that social conditions act as a drive to extraverts, and to the greater retest scores of Ryan and Kovacic's contact athletes who were good pain tolerators and presumably extraverted.

From the above evidence it would appear that Wikin could be measuring the same dimension as Eysenck and the Russian School. However, until a physiological basis is produced as an explanation of differences in perceptual style it would be premature to accept or reject such a view.

All the work reported so far concerns introversion, arousal, excitation and lowered sensory thresholds. It could also be argued that if arousal is synonymous with a high state of cortical facilitation then effector outputs should be greater for introverts than extraverts, when equal stimulation is given.

Rachman (1961) postulated that:—

... the increased cortical excitation of the introvert facilitates the execution of accurate, economic movements ... We might, therefore, expect that differences in efficiency between introvert and extravert groups will be inflated in tasks requiring confined and precise movements and diminished in tasks requiring gross bodily movements.

Eysenck also claims that introverts make less errors in fine motor skills because (a) they have fewer I.R.P.s, therefore, fewer errors. (b) greater cortical excitation leads to greater control in risk taking which is reflected in accuracy at the expense of speed. (c) the introvert conditions easier, including social conditioning. As accuracy is highly regarded in our society then the introvert will seek this at the expense of speed.

Brierley (1961) supports this view in showing that hysterics (extraverted neurotics) are characterised by low accuracy while dythymics (introverted neurotics) by low speed.

The following conclusions may be drawn from the evidence so far presented:

  i quick excitatory potential leads to greater cortical excitation, which leads to greater control of the lower centres, which is expressed as introverted behaviour.

  ii there is a specific cortical arousing system called the reticular system.

  iii individuals vary with regard to the sensitivity of this system.

  iv individuals with a low threshold level of reticular arousal will be disposed to quick excitatory potential and, therefore, to introverted behaviour.

  v individuals with a high threshold level of reticular arousal will be disposed to develop excitatory potential slowly and will, therefore, develop extraverted behaviour.

  vi extraverts will also develop reactive inhibition more quickly, more strongly and will dissipate it more slowly than introverts.

From this discussion of the causal aspect of introversion/extraversion it is possible to attempt an explanation of the conflicting results, reported by physical educationists regarding this factor of personality.

The case for a positive correlation between extraversion and performance in sport has been widely argued by Kane (1964), Warburton (1967) and others. The evidence presented in part I does not entirely support this contention. The following points arising from the data and supporting the postulated positive correlation are:

  i the extravert functions better at a high level of arousal—as in, say, top-class competitions.

  ii Extraverts will seek out situations of high arousal, e.g. games playing, because of their 'stimulus hunger'.

  iii As stimulation is mediated by other people, as in a games setting, it follows that 'stimulus hungry' extraverts will seek this situation.

  iv Extraverts perform better towards the 'gross' end of the fine skill-gross skill continuum. Sport is a situation offering practice of gross motor skills.

  v Extraverts can tolerate pain to a better degree than introverts. Pain, obviously, is an important factor in contact games and individual pursuits of high physical intensity. Games playing should, therefore, suit extraverts better.

  vi For extraverts social conditions act as a drive. Games playing is a social condition and should motivate the extravert to a greater degree than the introvert.

In contrast the following arguments can be raised for a positive correlation between introversion and athletic ability:

   i The introvert shows lower sensory thresholds which could be important in sport where it is often necessary to respond to reduced cues.

  ii Introverts perform better in fine motor skills where confined and precise movements are required. It is possible that such movement might be of greater importance than the gross skills in certain sports, say fencing or rifle shooting.

 iii Introverts are better in terms of vigilance, due to fewer I.R.P.s. In precision events such as rifle shooting fewer I.R.P.s. could theoretically make for greater consistency.

 iv Some sports, such as cross country running, which do not have the variety of tasks or change of display that, say, a team game has, could induce reactive inhibition. As this would be greater in extraverts they would have greater difficulty in maintaining consistency of effort.

  v Introverts condition more easily than extraverts. For this reason they introject the values of society more easily and see the goals which society holds in esteem. Thus the achievement motive tends to be higher in introverts.

 vi As society holds accuracy in esteem the introverts will tend to stress accuracy at the expense of speed, the reverse being true of extraverts.

 vii If one were to argue that some sports, say, cross country running, afford less sensory stimulation than, say rugby football, then introverts would find the former conditions more congenial.

viii Again, there are sports where 'action' in gross bodily terms is restricted, e.g. rifle shooting. Here the competitor lies on the butt for a long period of time often in unfavourable conditions, with little gross bodily movement. If the extravert is 'action-orientated' then this particular sport ought not to appeal. In a similar way, rock-climbing often demands close constricted movement.

 xi If Field Dependence can be associated with extraversion then the extraverts will be more socially compliant. This would suggest that the extravert might be influenced by his opponent more than would the introvert.

  x There is a little evidence to suggest that the greater cortical control of the introvert leads to greater control of risk taking. This could of course, be an asset or a drawback depending on whether the 'risks' taken by the extravert 'pay-off' which they must at some time do.

Thus, one cannot argue that all sports favour the extravert. Rather the advantage for the extravert will strike a balance with the advantages for the introvert, with the emphasis shifting from one to the other from sport to sport. It would also appear obvious that if a balance is struck between extraversion and introversion in each sport, because there are advantages and drawbacks to both, then one would not expect to find group means in any sport going to the extremes of the continuum.

A look at the results, listed on pages   to   of the 42 studies, in which the 16 P.F. has been used, will serve as a check on these assumptions. Assuming, roughly, that a score of 7 represents marked extraversion when compared to the population mean of 5.5 (i.e. 7 is approximately + 1 S.D.) then only three of the forty-two groups show marked extraversion. Conversely, there are groups showing introversion of corresponding intensity e.g. cross country (club standard) 4.4 rifle shooting (club standard) 4.3, and golfers (club standard) 4.7. Excluding the seven groups mentioned the mean scores of the remaining groups are on or around the hypothesised population mean.

Such results should rebutt any sweeping claims that extraversion is, ipso facto, an essential element of the games players' personality. This is further supported by the wide range of individual scores in any one group, suggesting that players with the 'wrong' extraversion/introversion emphasis manage to overcome their deficiency! Thus, the hypothesis relating extraversion to sport does not hold good in each and every sport and certainly not to all individual players.

References

ALLPORT, G.W. (1937). "Personality: a psychological interpretation." New York: Holt, Rinehart & Winston.

BAKAN, P. (1959). Extraversion-introversion and improvement in an auditory vigilance task. *Brit. J. Psychol.,* **50**, 328-332.

BAKAN, P., BELTON, J.A. & TOTH, J.C. (1963). Extraversion-introversion and decrement in an auditory vigilance task. In D.N. Buckner & J.J. McGrath (Eds.) "Vigilance: a symposium." New York' McGraw.

BARRETT, G.V., MCCABE, P.A. & THORNTON, C.L. (1967). Relation of perceptual style to measures of visual functioning. *Percept. Mot. Skills,* **25**, 235-236.

BILLS, A.G. (1931). Blocking: a new principle in mental fatigue. *Amer. J. Psychol.,* **43**, 230-245.

BLOOMBERG, M. (1965). Field independence-dependence and susceptibility to distraction. *Percept. Mot. Skills.,* **20**, 805-13.

BRIERLEY, M. (1961). The speed and accuracy characteristics of neurotics. *Brit. J. Psychol.,* **52**, 273-280.

BUTLER, M. (1929). Modern athletics. In Mason, M.G. (Ed.) Character and physical education. *Research Papers in P.E.,* **6,** 3-9.

BOULTON, S.M. (1966). Relationship beteen mental ability, physique and various activities of adolescent boys in a comprehensive school. *Research Papers in P.E.,* **3,** 3-13.

CATTELL, R.B. (1960). Some psychological correlates of physical fitness and physique. *Exercise and Fitness.* 138-150 Univ. of Illinois.

CATTELL, R.B. (1965). "The Scientific Analysis of Personality." Harmondsworth: Penguin.

CATTELL, R.B. & EBER, H.W. (1957). "Handbook for the 16 P.E. Questionnaire." Illinois: I.P.A.T.

CATTELL, R.B. & EBER, H.W. (1962). "Handbook for the 16 P.F. Questionnaire." Illinois: I.P.A.T.

CATTELL, R.B., EBER, H.W. & TATSUOKA, M.M. (1970). "Handbook for the 16 Personality Factor Questionnaire." Illinois: I.P.A.T.

CATTELL, R.B. & WARBURTON, F.W. (1961). Cross cultural comparisons of patterns of extraversion and anxiety. *Brit. J. Psychol.,* **52,** 3-15.

CHILD, D. (1964). The relationship between introversion, extraversion and neuroticism and performance in school examinations. *Brit. J. Ed. Psychol.,* **34,** 187-196.

CLARIDGE, G.S. (1960). The excitation-inhibition balance in neurotics. In H.H. Eysenck (Ed.) "Experiments in Personality. Vol. 2" New York:Praeger.

COCKERILL, I. (1968). Personality of golf players. Unpub. thesis, Univ. of Leeds Institute of Education.

COFER, C.N. & JOHNSON, W.R. (1960). Personality dynamics in relations to exercise and sports. In W.R. Johnson (Ed.) "Science and Medicine of Exercise and Sport." New York: Harper.

COLQUHOUN, W.P., & CORCORAN, P.W.T. (1964). The effects of time of day and social isolation on the relationships between temperament and performance. *Brit. J. Soc. Clin. Psychol.,* **3,** 226-231.

COSTELLO, C.G. & EYSENCK, H.J. (1961). Persistence, personality and motivation. *Percept. Mot. Skills,* **12,** 169-170.

DIALOGUE (1970). Miscellany. "Schools Council News Letter. No. 1" London: Schools Council Publication Co.

DUGGAN, A.S. (1937). A comparative study of undergraduate women majors and non-majors in P.E. with respect to certain personality traits. *Res. Quart.,* **8,** 3.

DUNSTONE, J.H. (1964). Effect of some personality variables on electrical vestibular stimulation. *Percept. Mot. Skills.,* **18,** 689-695.

EVANS, F.J. (1967). Field dependence and the Maudsley Personality Inventory. *Percept. Mot. Skills,* **24,** 526.

EYSENCK, H.J. (1955). Cortical inhibition, figural after-effects and theory of personality. *J. Abnorm. Soc. Psychol.,* **51,** 94-106.

EYSENCK, H.J. (1959). Personality and problem solving. *Psychol. Rep.,* **5,** 592.

EYSENCK, H.J. (1967). "Biological Basis of Personality." Springfield: Thomas.

FRENCH, J.D. (1957). The reticular formation. In "Psychobiology: readings from Scientific American (1966)." San Francisco: Freeman.

FURNEAUX, W.D. (1962). The psychologist and the university. In "Research and Experiment in Education." Dept. Educ., Newcastle University.

GRAY, J.A. (1968). The physiological basis of personality. *Adv. Sci.,* **24,** 119-122, and 293-305.

HALCOMB, C.G. & KIRK, R.E. (1965). Organismic variables as predictors of vigilance behaviour. *Percept. Mot. Skills,* **21,** 547-552.

HARDMAN, K. (1962). An investigation into the possible relationship between athletic ability and certain personality traits in 3rd year Secondary Modern School boys. Unpub. D.A.S.E. diss. University of Manchester.

HARDMAN, K. (1968). The personality differences between top class games players and players of lesser ability. Unpub. M.Ed. thesis, University of Manchester.

HENDRY, L.B. (1968). Assessment of the personality traits in the Coach - Swimmer relationship and a preliminary examination of the father figure stereotype. *Res. Quart.,* **39,** 543-551.

HEUSNER, W.V. (1952). Personality traits of champion and former champion athletes. Unpub. M.A. thesis. University of Illinois.

HOGAN, M.J. (1966). Influence of motivation on reactive inhibition in introversion/extraversion. *Percept. Mot. Skills,* **22,** 187-192.

HOVLAND, C.I. (1951). Human learning and retention. In S.S. Stevens (Ed.) "Handbook of Experimental Psychology." London: Livingstone.

HOWARTH, E. (1963). Some laboratory measures of introversion/extraverson. *Percept. Mot. Skills,* **17,** 55-60.

HULL, C.L. (1943). "Principles of Behaviour." New York: Appleton.

JACKSON, J. (1967). Personality and rock-climbing. Unpub. diss. University of Leeds Institute of Education.

JONES, C.M. (1968). "Tennis: how to become a champion." London: Faber.

KANE, J.E. (1962). Physique and physical abilities of fourteen year old boys in relation to personal and social adjustment. Unpub. M.Ed., thesis. University of Manchester.

KANE, J.E. (1964). Psychological correlates of physique and physical abilities. In E., Jokl & B. Simon (Eds.) "International Research in Sport and Physical Education." Illinois: Thomas.

KANE, J.E. (1966). Personality description of soccer ability. *Research in P.E.,* **1,** 54-64.

KEOGH, J. (1959). Relationship of motor ability and athletic participation in standardized personality measures. *Res. Quart.,* **30,** 438-445.

KROLL, W. (1967). Sixteen personality factor profiles of collegiate wrestlers. *Res. Quart.,* **38,** 49-57.

KROLL, W. & CARLSON, B.R. (1967). Discriminant function and hierarchial grouping analysis of karate participants. *Res. Quart.*, **38**, 405-11.

KROLL, W. & PETERSON, K.H. (1965). Personality factor profiles of collegiate football teams. *Res. Quart.*, **36**, 433-440

LE GROS CLERK (1936). The topography and homologies of the hypothalamic nuclei in man. *J. Anat.*, **70**, 203-215.

LEVINE, F.M. & TURSKY, B. (1966). Tolerance for pain, extraversion and neuroticism; failure to replicate results. *Percept. Mot. Skills, 23, 847-850.*

LONGLAND, J.L. (1955). Physical Education and character. *Phys. Rec.*, **7**, 7-11.

LOVATT EVANS, C. (1949). "Principles of Human Physiology." London: Churchill.

LYNN, R. & EYSENCK, H.J. (1961). Tolerance for pain, extraversion and neuroticism. *Percept. Mot. Skills*, **12**, 161-162.

MARSHALL, F.J.C. (1949). "Physical Activities for Boys' Schools." London: U,L.P.

MASON, M.G. (1968). Character and physical education. *Research Papers in P.E.*, **6**, 3-9.

MCINTOSH, P.C. (1966). Mental ability and success in sport. *Research in Physical Education*, **1**, 20-27.

OLTMAN, P.K. (1964). Field dependence and arousal. *Percept. Mot. Skills*, **19**, 441.

OTTO, W. (1965). Inhibition potential in good and poor achievers. *J. Educ. Psychol.*, **56**, 200-207.

PALMER, J. (1933). Personal qualities of women teachers of physical education. *Res. Quart.*, **4**, 31-48.

PAVLOV, I.P. (1927). "Conditioned Reflexes." Oxford: University Press.

PERRIN, F.A.C., (1921). An experimental study of motor ability. *J. Exp. Psychol.*, **4**, 24-56.

PETRIE, A. (1967). "Individuality in Pain and Suffering: the reducer and the augmenter." Chicago: University Press.

POSER, E. (1960). Proc. of the XVth Int. Congress of Exp. Psychol. Bonn. In, H.J. Eysenck (1967). "Biological Basis of Personality." Springfield: Thomas.

RACHMAN, S. (1961). Psychomotor behaviour and personality with special reference to conflict. Unpub. Ph.D. thesis, University of London.

RANKIN, E.F. (1963). Reading test performance of introverts and extraverts. *12th Year Book Nat. Reading Conf.*

REED, G.F. (1961). Audiometer response consistency, auditory fatigue and personality. *Percept. Mot. Skill*, **12**, 126.

REED, G.F. & MCKENNA, T.C. (1964). Personality and time estimation in sensory deprivation. *Percept. Mot. Skills*, **18**, 182.

ROSSI, A.M. & SALMON, P. (1965). Note on the reactions of extraverts and introverts to sensory deprivation. *Percept. Mot. Skills*, **20**, 1183.

RUSHALL, B.S. (1967). Personality profiles and a theory of behaviour modification for swimmers. *Swimming Technique,* October, 66-71

RYAN, E.D. & KOVACIC, C.R. (1966). Pain tolerance and athletic participation. *Percept. Mot. Skills,* **22**, 383-390.

SINCLAIR, E.D. (1968). Personality and rugby football. Unpub. thesis, Univ. of Leeds Institute of Education.

SMITH, S.L. (1966). The effect of personality and drugs on auditory threshold when risk taking factors are controlled. In H.J. Eysenck (1967). "Biological Basis of Personality." Springfield: Thomas.

SOLAR, D. & DAVENPORT, G. (1964). Social compliance as a function of field dependence. *Percept. Mot. Skills,* **19**, 229-306.

SPIELMAN, J. (1963). The relation between personality and the frequency and duration of involuntary rest pauses during massed practice. Unpub. Ph.D. thesis. University of London.

STANDISH, R.R. & CHAMPION, R.A. (1960). Task difficulty and drive in verbal learning. *J. Exp. Psychol.,* **59**, 361-365.

SWEENEY, D.R. & FINE, B.J. (1965). Pain reactivity and field dependence. *Percept. Mot. Skills,* **21**, 757-758.

THULIN, J.G. (1947). "Gymnastics Handbook." Lund: Swedish Gymnastic Institute.

TRANEL, N. (1962). Effects of perceptual isolation on introverts and extraverts. *Psychiat. Res.,* **1**, 185-192.

WARBURTON, F.W. (1967). The relationship between personality characteristics and sporting ability. *Proc. Brit. Soc. Sport. Psychol.,* Manchester.

WHITING, H.T.A. & HENDRY, L. B. (1969). A study of international table tennis players. Unpub. memorandum. In H.T.A. Whiting (1969) "Acquiring Ball Skill." London; Bell.

WITKIN, H.A., DYK, R.B., FATERSON, D.R. & KARP, S.A. (1962). "Psychological Differentiation." New York: Wiley.

THE 'PHYSICAL EDUCATIONIST' STEREOTYPE

by L. B. Hendry

Introduction

The role of the teacher of physical education is shaped in part by the expectations of individuals with whom he interacts in his social environment. Their perceptions of, and reactions to him, may have an effect on his subsequent behaviour patterns. His own personality may also influence, to some extent, how he performs his teaching role in schools, but this is reinforced by the expectations attached to the role.

This chapter sets out to examine some of the existing evidence about the physical educationist mainly in terms of his personality characteristics but also seeking to explain how the expectations of other social actors and his own role perceptions may affect his school-function. The examination of findings is conducted, loosely, within a theoretical framework of *stereotype*. The limitations of this approach are indicated and should be clearly noted. For example, the physical education teacher is often portrayed as a muscular, dominant, stable, not overtly bright individual, which, of course, may not be an accurate picture of many members of the profession.

What is a Stereotype?

Linton (1936) suggested that any position in society carries with it a status—'a collection of rights and duties'—and in this way role can be explained as behaviour oriented to the patterned expectations of others. This is so because as Mead (1934) postulated some time ago, self is built up through interaction with others, by 'projecting' oneself to be enabled to perceive self through the eyes and attitudes of others in one's social environment. More recently Westwood (1967) has defined role as playing different parts at different times in differing circumstances, suggesting that within each role the actor's behaviour will conform broadly to how other people conceive the role performance to be.

Thus, given individual personality differences, there will be a degree of predictability in social behaviour. Roles may give rise to stereotypes and stereotypes may be closely associated with roles. While roles are norms associated with differences of function *among* group-members, stereotypes are norms related to the group as a whole. So stereotypes indicate variables which distinguish *between* groups: they are a simplification, categorized in terms of attributes common to the groups that fall within the parameters, ignoring individual differences between them.

Groups are often defined by generalisations about the behaviour or personality characteristics of members; or even by reference to certain physical qualities of the group. Categorization by stereotype is one of the basic social processes, and is absolutely essential in ordering the environment, and of enabling an individual to develop a 'self-image' better to understand his position in that environment. Stereotypes can often be inadequate exaggerated and distorted beliefs which persist about a group, but this is because of inadequacies of the criteria used to define a particular stereotype, and cannot be avoided.

In relation to the individual an essential function of the stereotype is that of a reference group[1] contributing significantly to the individual's concept of self (one of man's abilities is to be able to regard himself as an object so that it can be described not only by others but by 'self' (Mead, 1934)). 'Self' can best be explained in terms of categories to which it may belong: physical, personality, stereotype categories, and those part-stereotypes based on roles. This 'image' the individual has of himself enables comparison with others and provides a model for conduct in many relations with other people.

Social Stereotypes

Kiker & Miller (1967) have argued that the perception of personality characteristics or temperamental variables of strangers based on first impressions is a common experience with important social and personal implications, and that many of these impressions may be based on facial expression, physical appearance, gesture and style of dress. Their findings suggested that charismic stereotypes in terms of physique also exist. McClelland (1953) reported similar findings. American college students corresponding certain somatotype silhouettes to identify personality types showed that the mesomorphic stereotype was seen as being socially and personally favourable, while the ectomorphic stereotype was seen as being socially submissive and personally unfavourable (Dibiase

---

[1] Reference groups are groups with which the individual compares in evaluating status (Hyman 1960).

& Hjelle 1968). In a similar way, Sleet (1969) found that stereotyped social images of individuals based on physique existed among middle-aged men. In his study of adolescent boys Flanagan (1951) showed that mesomorphic adolescent males were subjectively rated by their peers as 'real boys' and 'sporting'.

Sheldon (1942) had earlier postulated reasons for this acceptance of social stereotypes—that of socially mediated stereotypes of behaviour in our culture for individuals of a particular somatotype. Methods of measuring actual body size against a given scale and hence classifying into types had been devised by Sheldon (1940) and later Parnell (1958). Sheldon & Stevens (1942) also assigned various personality traits to the various types of build. Although psychologists have not entirely agreed with Sheldon & Stevens (1942) temperament-physique relationship (e.g. Sugarman & Haronian, 1964), studies by Brodsky (1954), McCandless (1960) and Wells & Seigel (1961) have shown that the social desirability of personality stereotypes based on physique came out more or less as Sheldon & Stevens (1942) had originally suggested. The concordance of stereotyped female physiques using males as judges has also been demonstrated by Miller & Stewart (1968).

Throughout society certain stereotypes produce particular effects and re-actions:--

> The fat child, like to thin,
> learns that the playground
> gives rewards to the mesomorph
> not to him.
> (Allport, 1961).

It has been shown how adolescent boys felt the need to appear in a favourable light socially even in the face of very obvious physical defects; obviously males desire to be accepted by society more than females and feel that they are so accepted (Meissner, Thoreson & Butler, 1967).

Stereotypes in an athletic context have been investigated and it can be suggested in general that physical education students reveal similarities of physique, personality and cognitive style with team athletes. Additionally, their teacher training environment and interest in physical activities, their selection procedure, their physical prowess point towards the possibility that they share a number of communalities of personal characteristics with athletes (see p. 78-80).

The mass media (films, T.V., magazines, etc.) tend to show the physical educationist as a muscular, dominant, aggressive, sociable individual—a man of action rather than words, and Willgoose (1961) has suggested that physical games are the invention of the mesomorphic man. So the important question may now be asked:—

'Is the teacher of physical education a different "type" from his classroom colleagues?'

'The Physical Educationist' Stereotype (Indicatory Evidence)

The status of physical education teachers is seen to be lower than that of teachers of academic subjects (Musgrove & Taylor 1969), and this lower status is clearly perceived by physical education students during training (Appleby 1967). In addition, Lee (1968) has indicated that physical education students consider their teaching function to be mainly in the area of social education, and this is substantiated by Heaton's (1969) study.

Writing about female physical education teachers, Cannon (1964) suggested that their isolated, rather self-contained training contributes to their 'alienation' from other members of staff. Male physical education students more often undergo training within a general college campus, along with students following a variety of general teaching courses, but may be alienated by the nature of their course with its emphasis on personal physical ability and methodology. General (academic) students have already embarked upon courses where there is greater emphasis on subject matter and subject specialisation—and academic specialisation is rewarded by society (Wilson 1962).

At the interview stage, before acceptance for college is finalised, a difference in selection between specialist physical education students at 'wing' course colleges and general students is apparent (Hendry 1969). In addition to interview procedures, the physical education student is usually given a test of physical ability and is expected to reveal a high level of physical or sporting expertise (for example, being a county standard athlete). Perhaps this is a necessary aspect of selection procedure for a subject that has no school leaving examinations which other subjects no doubt 'use' as an aid to selection for teacher training courses and university entrance.

Accepting these differences in approach to selecting students, and in the structure and emphasis of the specialist physical education teachers' course, do physical education students differ from general course students in personal characteristics or in academic or social class background?

The average age of male college students in England is 21.5 years (Statistics of Education, 1963), and Whitehead (1966) has written that physical education students tend to be younger than general students in training. This means, on average, they spend less time in the sixth form.

The *Report on Entry to Colleges of Education (1967)* stated that men accepted at colleges of education with two or more 'a' level passes as a percentage of total entry was:—

1965   1966

38.4%   37.5%

A study by Hargreaves (1968) showed that the percentage of male students attending nine 'wing' colleges of physical education (1966) entry who gained two or more 'A' level passes at G.C.E. examinations was 47.54%. The approximate numbers of initial applicants received by these colleges numbered more than 3,000.

In social class the parents of the physical education students in Whitehead's (1966) sample were shown to be 53.2% in Groups I and II (Registrar General's Classification) whereas only 45.8% of the general course students used as a control group were in Groups I and II. The majority of teachers come from Groups II and III, and are lower middle class (Banks 1968). It would seem then that specialist physical education students show some differences in academic qualifications and social class background from student colleagues with whom they will work in schools on completion of their college courses and these social and academic differences are minimally 'in favour' of physical education students.

Parnell (1958) has commented that it is the muscular student who participates in outdoor pursuits and games. A comparison of the somatotypes of Commonwealth physical education students with students on physical education courses at English Colleges, was carried out by Carter (1964). In his findings he indicated that all samples shared similar trends, with the mesomorphic component predominating. He concluded that high mesomorphy is positvely selective, while markedly high endomorphy and ectomorphy are negatively selective for physical education students.

Sheldon & Stevens (1942) has suggested considerable relationship between somatotype components and temperament (though their findings have been criticised), and Carter (1964) considered that it would seem reasonable to expect that many of the temperamental traits of somatonia, which Sheldon & Stevens (1942) found correlated highly with mesomorphy, would characterise many teachers of physical education.

> Such traits as assertiveness of posture and movement, love of physical adventure, need and enjoyment of exercise, love of dominating, bold directness of manner, competitive aggressiveness, physical courage for combat, and spartan indifference to pain may readily be observed in many physical education teachers.

Individuals who are attracted towards teaching physical education differ in physique from those of other occupations. The suggestion has been that whilst individuals in other occupations cover the whole somatochart, physical education students and 'athletes' tend towards the mesomorphic area of the chart. Such findings have led Carter (1964) to suggest that physical education students may well be chosen in the image of those carrying out the selection. Carter (1964) has further postulated that physical education students do not have the mesomorphic sector of the somatochart entirely to themselves. He showed that there were striking similarities between his samples and the somatotypes of outstanding athletes and concluded that the reason may well be that individuals are attracted towards a career in physical education because of their interest and success in physical activities. Therefore, to the extent that teachers choosing physical education are outstanding athletes, then career and physique appear to be related. The more selective the sport is in terms of physique, the less relationship there will be between somatotypes and physical education samples. Tappen (1950), Cureton (1951) Eranko & Karvonen (1955) among others have shown a relationship between somatotype groupings and champion athletes and Smithells & Cameron (1962) have made the general observation that while all sorts of body-type have been successful in all walks of life in our society, those drawn to physical education as a career tend to have common characteristics—in particular being mesomorphic—and certain builds are almost never attracted to the profession.

It also appears that Sheldon & Stevens' (1942) theories on the temperament/physique relationship led Parnell (1958) to state that physical education teachers may have a problem in acquiring a comprehensive outlook if their physique and 'training culture' deprive them of 'inborn' understanding of two-thirds of their pupils of different somatotype. So although physique and temperament have provided success and interest in physical activities, there are built-in dangers of teaching blindly an unstated philosophy of 'you too can be like me!' (Smithells & Cameron 1962).

Women physical education students appear to differ less from their population means on endomorphy and ectomorphy than do the men. Bale's (1969) study on 150 students at a specialist physical education college, and comparisons with earlier surveys showed that both men and women physical education students are more muscular and less endomorphic than general students. He further postulated that as mesomorphy is related to athletic ability physical education students are attracted to their profession because of an interest and success in physical activities. Carter (1965) also concluded that it was the higher scoring on the mesomorphic component that distinguished the women physical education student from other college women. Like their male counterparts, he stated, they usually enjoy exercise, physical adventure and athletic competition. They tend to be extraverted, assertive, direct in manner, and physically courageous. The physique and personality of women physical education teachers may make them insensitive to the child with a more delicate or heavy build with little physical ability or athletic drive (Bale, 1969). Thus the relationship between body-type and temperament may have some relevance in the physical education teacher's approach to teaching interactions with pupils.

Kane (1968) investigated male and female college students (both general course and physical education specialists), in terms of the relationship between personality, as measured by Cattell's (1957) 16 Personality Factor Inventory, and physical ability (Fleishman, 1964). His results showed that extraversion and stability, together with Fleishman's (1964) test of 16 physical factors, accounted for 20% of the total variance. While his findings indicated little relationship within criterion groups, there were relationships within sex groupings. In males, extraversion was associated with physical ability, stability with explosive strength, tough-mindedness (factor I) with muscular strength, and conservatism (factor Q1) with endurance.

Earlier studies by Palmer (1933), Duggan (1937) and Espenschade (1948) looked at the personality of women physical education students. All the studies found physical education students to be extraverted, stable and dominant.

In studying the personality of first year male physical education students Kane (1965) showed that as a group they deviated markedly from the population mean in surgency (factor F), realism (factor I), and to some extend in sociability (factor A), adventurousness (factor H) and will-power (factor Q3). They were significantly higher than general students on extraversion, whereas they tended to be lower on anxiety. Whiting (1966) conducted a similar investigation of 22 physical education teachers (mean age 30 years) following an advanced course of study. Within a wide range of scores, they approximated as a group towards the population mean on extraversion, while their anxiety score was lower. Brooke (1967) also found that physical education students tended to be highly extraverted.

In Kane's (1968) study the outstanding personality traits of male physical education students were dominance (factor E), realism (factor I), confidence (factor O), and low nervous tension (factor Q4). In addition there were no significant personality changes over three years of teacher training: male and female physical education students revealing personality similarities. There were greater differences between physical education and general students; stability and extraversion being the important differentiators. Kane's (1968) study also showed, (contrary to earlier findings), that there was no significant relationship between physique and total personality in general course students or specialist physical education students near the completion of their courses, though the physical education students were found to be mesomorphic. In the male criterion groups tough-minded extraversion was seen to be related to general athletic ability, and dominance (factor E), group dependency (factor Q2) and low nervous tension (factor Q4) with sports participation.

In a study on personality characteristics in three groups of physical educationists-undergraduates, graduates and teachers Thorpe (1958) used Edwards' Personal Preference Schedule (1953). In addition, this study compared total group means with the published norms. It was found that a similar pattern in personality did exist among the experimental groups, and that they differed from the Edwards' Personal Preference Schedule (E.P.P.S.) norms in a number of scales. They were higher on deference, order, dominance and endurance, while being lower on autonomy, succourance (seeking help), nurturance (giving help), heterosexuality and aggression. Locke (1962) found a similar homogeneity with a group of male physical education teachers. The only E.P.P.S. variables on which they differed from a comparable group of general teachers were succourance, nurturance and affiliation. In addition, in each case there were higher scores than the sample of women physical educationists (Thorpe 1958).

However, these mean scores were pertinent only to the study or the norms being used and in fact, based on the Edwards' Personal Preference Schedule, male and female physical educationists had profiles characterised by a small amount of intra-group variance. Both groups appears to be group reliant, authoritarian, dominant, but not aggressive.

Amongst others Haverland (1957) has indicated the crucial factors associated with the personality pattern of more successful teachers are sociability (factor A), emotional stability (factor C), conscientiousness (factor G) and willpower (factor Q3), all of which should be high. The sample of physical education students investigated by Kane (1965) had scores significantly above the mean on the first and last factors, but approximated to the general population mean on the other two factors. The profile similarity coefficient[2] between Haverland's (1957) findings and Kane's (1965) sample was moderately high (r_p = + 0.67).

At this stage it seems reasonable to suggest that certain evidence does exist to indicate that male students of physical education differ from other college students in academic qualifications and social class, and are differentiated by somatotype (being markedly more mesomorphic), which may predispose them towards physical activities (Parnell 1958) and this in turn may direct them towards a particular career within the teaching profession.

Again, certain personality characteristics seem to distinguish them from other students, namely, sociability, dominance, realism and stability.

Musgrave (1965) has stated that though teachers generally may have a definite role, they do not go through a special selection or moulding process as a result of playing this role, and so there would not appear to be a distinct and consistent teaching personality. It is arguable that Musgrave's (1965) statement about teacher training is not so applicable to students of physical education at specialist or 'wing' colleges, who *may* be put through a moulding process. In addition, certain physique and temperamental 'types' may be attracted towards such a regimen. Here it should be remembered that Kane (1968) found no significant changes in personality spanning the three-year college period, and Oliver (1956) has indicated that a general teaching factor, knowledge of subject-matter, and personal-emotional qualities were important attributes in teaching physical education. Additionally, there were no significant differences shown in these attributes between male and female physical educationists.

If particular physical and personality characteristics are evident in students of physical education then it is possible that this in turn would affect their attitude and approach to teaching, and their social skills. The suggestion here is that if certain 'types' (in terms of physique and personality) with sporting interests and physical ability go through a teacher training process different from general

---

[2]Profile similarity coefficient is the matching of two profiles to examine the closeness of one to the other, and is analogous to a correlation coefficient (Cattell & Eber 1957).

course students, then this process, allied to their own physical and temperamental pre-disposition, may produce teachers given to certain stereotyped social
responses and teaching attitudes which will reveal themselves in a number of
ways. In particular their teaching approach will differentiate them from others
who have followed general college courses.

Research inter-relating Eysenck's (1947) Cattell (1946) and Witkin et al's
(1954) theories of personality with physique have shown conflicting results.
Sugerman & Haronian (1964) have related mesomorphic body-type to field
independence, while Evans (1967) found positive correlations between field
dependency and extraversion. This seems linked to Eysenck's (1965) postulations on the need of extraverts for social field dependence. The general,
subjective view of the mesomorph, however, (supported by Sheldon & Stevens
(1942) claims) is of an extraverted individual, with a predisposition towards
movement behaviour (Willgoose, 1961) and with the possibility of a highly
developed sophistication of body-concept because of the variety of movement
experience (Witkin, 1962)

The 'Physical Educationist' Stereotype

These conflicting ideas and findings led Hendry (1970) to investigate criterion
groups of final year male physical education students and general course
students to examine possible differences in physique, personality, social responses and teaching attitudes and to examine relationships between personality,
physique, and attitude to teaching in these criterion groups. The test battery
consisted of the Eysenck Personality Inventory (1964), the 16 P.F.I. (Cattell &
Eber, 1957) and the Dynamic Personality Inventory (Grygier 1961) as well as
tests of social response, perceptual set (Witkin et al, 1962), teaching attitude and
measure of physique (Parnell, 1958). In Hendry's (1970) study physical
education students were found to be younger than general students, thus
supporting the findings of Whitehead (1966) that physical education students
generally commence their teacher training course at an earlier age than general
course students, after spending less time in sixth form.

Not surprisingly, the physical educationists were shown to be more muscular,
which is in line with other studies (Smithells & Cameron, 1962; Tanner, 1964;
Kane, 1968). A more authoritarian attitude to teaching was revealed by the
physical educationists, though both sets of scores fell within the reported range
of attitude scores for British teachers of some years experience (Evans 1969).
Certain aspects of the male physical education teachers' work may call for a
more direct and authoritarian manner and this could well be reflected in their
scores at student level. While the modern approach to the teaching of educational gymnastics is informal and flexible, safety precautions related to the
teaching of athletics, trampolining, swimming, vaulting and agility all necessitate

teacher-direction. The ethos surrounding teacher-training systems at particular colleges may also have an effect in creating particular attitudes to teaching. As Evans (1969) has pointed out, teaching attitudes are susceptible to training.

On the basis of the Test of Social Insight (Cassell 1963) physical education students were found to be highly competitive and aggressive, and revealed poor social insight. Sheldon & Stevens (1942) postulated that mesomorphy would correlate with such social traits as love of dominating, bold directness of manner and competitive aggressiveness. It has been pointed out by Skinner (1953) that competition exists in social situations when the behaviour of one individual is reinforced only with the loss of reinforcement to another individual, hence the dominant, muscular physical educationist needing social approval and reward may seek such reinforcement aggressively—this apparently being his mode of social response. This lends some support to Eysenck's (1947) definition of the typical extravert:—

> . . . tends to be aggressive, and loses his temper quickly, his feelings are not kept under tight control.

The results from Eysenck's (1964) Personality Inventory, and the 16 P.F.I. (Cattell & Eber 1957) showed that the physical education students were significantly more stable and extraverted than their general college colleagues. In several of Cattell & Eber's (1957) primary factors which contribute to second-order extraversion and stability, physical educationists had significantly higher scores. These findings are mirrored by Brooke's (1967) investigation of specialist physical education students and Carr's (1970) findings on Scottish Specialist physical education students. The evidence for the existence of a physical education stereotype is further enhanced when Kane's (1968) findings—where he showed no canonical variate to significantly discriminate between the male and female criterion groups—were compared by Jones (1970) with her own sample of 140 women specialist students, and other specialist samples, in terms of their personality profile similarity coefficients. In all cases the coefficient was higher than + 0.90. Because Hendry's (1970) investigation utilised British norms for the 16 P.F.I. (Warburton 1969) it was only possible to convert and compare Jones' (1970) raw scores. The profile similarity coefficient in this case was + 0.86, giving much support to a stereotypic personality profile for specialist physical education students, both male and female.[3]

In comparing the specialist students with the samples of general college students on the many sub-scales of the Dynamic Personality Inventory (Grygier

---

[3]It is not of course suggested that *all* physical education teachers are of similar 'type'— obviously there *is* a range of individual differences—nevertheless consistent trends exist.

1961),[4] several significant differences were apparent. The picture that emerged of physical educationists was of aggressive yet sociable individuals. They liked social activities and sought social roles. To this end they were concerned with their clothes and general appearance. It is possible that traditions of the college with which they were associated also influenced this aspect of their make-up. It was shown that they enjoy the attention and admiration of others.

While as a group physical education students were sociable, they were also aggressive—verbally and intellectually—showing self-assertive behaviour. Linked to this was a higher achievement drive, a strong emphasis on authority (to which they were submissive) and discipline.

Aggression and drive for achievement may have in part accounted for the impulsiveness, emotional expressiveness shown, and their interest in activity and sense of adventure. Physical educationists also showed a tendency to plan, manage and organise. As a group they had a high masculine sexual identification. They showed an interest in objects of phallic symbolic significance which may be interpreted as some form of self-identity relating to their high masculinity rating. They were also shown to be masculine in their social orientation in terms of roles, attitudes, and interests.

Witkin et al (1962) have postulated that extensive movement experience may help in the development of body sophistication, and Sugerman & Haronian (1964) have also suggested that involvement in 'athletic' pursuits may have a direct effect on body-image, a more defined concept of body boundaries, and a more effective, economical use of the body. It may be reasonable to expect such individuals to reveal this development of body-concept in their drawings (which Witkin et al, 1962, claim is a method of assessing body-sophistication). Unfortunately this was not clarified by Hendry's (1970) study, but Witkin et al (1962) have argued the development of body concept may be relatively stable by early adulthood; general course students can avail themselves of movement experiences (especially games and sports) within intra- and extra-mural college physical activities programmes. These findings to some extend would support Bell's (1969) contention that movement courses do not enable physical education students to reveal a more sophisticated body-concept (in Witkin's terms) than general students. (Bell's, 1969, samples were not in fact following a specialist course but were following a physical education *main* course.)

The Embedded Figures Test (Witkin et al 1962) showed that physical education students were more field independent than other students, but not significantly so, and both sets of scores fell within the range of scores derived from American student samples. Jones (1970) has shown that specialist women

---

[4] Because of the terminology used to describe the scales in this psycho-sexual inventory no attempt is made here to identify the scales, in other than everyday terms. The reader is advised to consult D.P.I. Handbook (N.F.E.R.) for information.

physical education students were significantly more field independent than American women students. As it has been reported that women are more field dependent than men Jones' (1970) findings are of some importance. In relation to Hendry's (1970) investigation it is noted that male students are enabled to involve themselves in (and may be interested in) games, whereas women students, because of cultural pressures, may not be so encouraged to 'athletic' participation and, therefore, the movement opportunities offered to women physical education students may enable them to reveal greater field independence and vice versa.

Component Patterns and Pattern Discrimination

While the reported significant differences discussed above give a picture of the 'physical educationist' stereotype of broadening proportions in terms of its social significance, these findings only tell a limited amount about how these differences are associated. Comparison of the component 'loadings' accounting for a major percentage of the variance in the physical education students group revealed that there was a social role-seeking component containing both yielding and aggressive characteristics, one which linked Eysenck's (1947) extraversion with a number of Cattell's (1946) factors, and certain social traits from the psycho-sexual variables. Another component associated competitiveness with poor social insight, and yet another indicated aggressive authoritarianism.

The 'loadings' in the general student sample showed apparent basic differences—conventionality, self-effacement, good social insight accounting for a major percentage of the variance.

By the use of a discriminant analysis (Ahmavaara 1954) the component patterns were scrutinised in a relatively objective way. Results indicated that there *were* essential differences between the component patterns of the two groups. In most cases the pattern communalities ran in opposite directions, extraversion v. introversion, stability v. neuroticism, competitive aggression v. good social insight. Hence, there *are* clearly differences in patterns of psychological associated variables between physical education students and students following other courses, which would clearly orient their particular social response and the interpretation of their separate teaching roles.

The physical educationist being apparently stable, extravert, competitive and authoritarian, all the evidence so far would support and extend the findings on the existence of an extraverted, muscular, authoritarian 'stereotype'. The most vital aspect of these findings may be in relation to social interaction, and particularly their implications for teaching: the evidence pointing to clear-cut dissimilarities between physical education and other college students.

Adorno et al (1950) have outlined the main characteristics of the authoritarian personality as possessing a strong tendency to conform, rather inflexible in thinking, and to having a dependence on authority. One might surmise that this 'type' would require a highly predictable environment with little uncertainty, ambiguity or innovation and change. There would be a rigid adherence to stereotype norms and possibly a sacrifice of the development of uniquely individual characteristics. Thus the authoritarian personality may have an unrealistically oversimplified perception of himself and of his social environment—being increasingly dependent on stereotype norms as a guide to behaviour and deviating little from these norms. He would not have learned the important social skill of equating individuality with conformity: of being an individual in his own right and yet being sufficiently predictable to enable him to form reasonable social interactions in the existing society. There is also the possibility that in dealing with younger people the authoritarian personality will contribute to their development along similar lines; treating the child as an exemplar of a stereotype rather than an individual, perhaps handicapping the child by the clarity and restrictions of the expected norms within their social milieu:

> The lack of an individualised approach to the child . . . as well as a tendency to transmit mainly a set of conventional rules and customs may be considered as interfering with the development of a clear-cut personal identity in the growing child. (Adorno et al 1950).

In addition there is another implication in that there may be greater identification and affinity for children in whom there are clearly developed signs that they are indeed exemplars of the stereotype, and by implication a neglect of children who do not conform to this 'desired' social image.

Possible Educational Implications of the Stereotype

Having looked at the authoritarian personality in the social situation, what then are the implications of the cited research findings and personal postulations and speculations in relation to education and the educational system now and in the near future? Is it possible to suggest from the evidence on stereotypes a particular function and role performance?

The difference between role playing (i.e. performing the functions of a role) which is sociological and involves one in a whole set of behaviours and role taking (i.e. empathetic activity of placing oneself in the other's place in order to gain insights) which is psychological have been discussed. Coutu (1951) suggested that role taking is an important tool for the teacher. It may be asked if it is possible for the authoritarian to 'project' and, have empathy, especially with those unlike himself in temperament and physique?

In discussing the role of the teacher Musgrave (1965) considered that role is a two-way concept. It covers the set of values and expectations of a particular position in the social system from the point of view of both the occupant of the position and those with whom he interacts. It would seem that the role which is played by the teacher will be dependent not only on the teaching situation but also upon his background, intellectual capacity and type of training; personality and character will also affect the role which is played, since this undoubtedly influences the way in which the teacher's role is interpreted.

A study of women physical educationists indicated low status because the physical education teacher is seen as anti-academic, non-graduate, representing the physical, not particularly verbally articulate or interested in ideas. The job itself seems relatively easy with no marking, playing games, and evident enjoyment of jumping about because the teacher is still adolescent! Nevertheless, Cannon (1964), outlining the expectations of the institution, showed the role requirement in broad categories—these role requirements fell into such functions as promoter of physical exercise, organiser, a good physical performer, an aesthetic and medical auxillary. These requirements may be applicable to all the profession, male as well as female. Percival (1967) pointed critically at the physical aspect of teacher training:—

> Time after time with physical education students and with young teachers I have been impressed by their agility, skill and keenness to teach the able games player or gymnastic performer; rarely have I seen those whose feeling for the importance of their subject and imagination and human sympathy renders them willing and able to draw out and encourage the fat, the lazy, the awkward, the flat-footed, and the physically shy and retarded. Do we not spend too much time in producing good performers and too little on producing good teachers?

Yet entrants to physical education colleges are as academically well qualified as other college students (e.g. Hargreaves 1968), though perhaps less so than university undergraduates, so it may well be the conception of the physical nature of the subject—and hence the use of a stereotype—that separates the physical educationist from other teachers; the subject matter and the personality of the exemplars of the type blend to produce separation from other teachers. Scotland (1964) wrote that the physical education man is:—

> Generally a man of action rather than mind, a good man to play golf with, but not first choice for a discussion of professional problems.

Both Percival (1967) and Cannon (1964) have pointed out that physical education teachers are selected from midde, lower middle or upper working class strata where strategy and power games are encouraged (Sutton-Smith & Roberts 1963). Generally these claims match Whitehead's (1966) findings of students selected more often from the middle-class stratum of society. It seems possible that teachers of physical education emerge as different from their staff-room colleagues not only in teacher training, physique, temperament and social response, but also in terms of their social class background with, quite likely, a differing value system. Musgrave (1965) has proposed three 'ideal' types of teacher—the academic who teaches a subject, the child-centred teacher who teaches children, and the 'missionary' who sees his role as rescuing the child from his environment. Teachers may have differing role emphasis often resulting from their initial training. Perhaps because of the reasons advanced above the physical educationist perceives his role as the second type or even as the 'missionary' teacher. Certainly Lee's (1968) findings show a strong bias towards social education by the teacher of physical education. Part of the physical educationist's role may be seen as attempting to influence the behaviour patterns (character?) of pupils within the P.E. programme.

What are the qualities a teacher should possess? Wilson (1962) pointed out that warmth of personality and effective concern for children were implicit in the role, and moreover:—

> Role performance is a living process in which the establishment of rapport, the impact of personality are necessary to the stirring of the imagination and the awakening of enthusiasm involved in the learning process.

Obviously Wilson (1962) considers personal qualities to be important in the performance of the teacher's role. Taylor (1965) on the other hand has shown that children evaluated most highly being taught to take advantage of 'life chances'. The majority of teachers, according to Taylor (1965) evaluated most highly the good teacher's personal qualities, particularly patience, kindness, sympathy and understanding.

On both counts the physical educationist may 'miss out' for he is not a purveyor of 'life chances' via examinations, nor, according to the evidence is he likely to be particularly patient, understanding or have good social insight, but to some extent shows aggressive, assertive, domineering personality characteristics (Hendry, 1970). The suggestion in all this is that the physical educationist is, by his physique and personality, in danger of severely limiting his mode and scope of social interaction, particularly in the realm of teaching pupils. Parnell (1958), Smithells & Cameron (1962) and Carter (1964) have all pointed out the possible teaching limitations of this mesomorphic, stable, extraverted stereotype.

Whitehead (1969) in an extensive survey of the actual content of work in all the male specialist physical education colleges in Britain and a representative sample of boys' secondary schools, found an extremely limited curriculum despite current trends in educational thought and practice. In brief his findings were that although the layman may consider that great strides have been taken in physical education in recent years, the actual content of schools' programmes has changed little. Although the Board of Education in its syllabus of Physical

Training for Schools (1933) recommended that schools programmes for outdoor lessons should not be confined to soccer, rugby, cricket, hockey and athletics these activities are still included as the major portion of the time allocated for outdoor work. In addition there is not a large element of choice for boys in secondary schools' physical education programmes. Contrary to general trends of individual experience, exploration and invention male teachers of physical education spend only a very small portion of their time teaching educational gymnastics and modern educational dance. This reaction of the physical education practitioner begins to 'make more sense' when the evidence on the stereotype is reviewed. Is this not the typical behaviour pattern of the authoritarian personality with his dislike of change, and innovation; his conformity, inflexibility and rigid adherence to established behavioural norms, and a traditional pattern of existence?

Cannon (1964) and Percival (1967) considered that physical educationists are isolationists, having first attended a specialist or wing college, most often mixed only with other specialists and when teaching are further isolated because the gymnasium, games field and swimming pool are physically separated from the main school block. Countless other duties and responsibilities seem in many cases to keep the physical education teacher out of contact with other members of staff, and thus they are cut off from the main body of teachers. Perhaps this role is determined to an extent by the physical educationist himself and often isolation is self-inflicted. These exemplars of the stereotype, whilst being gregarious and socially stimulus-hungry, also possess an aggressively dominant mode of social response: one, it could be suggested, that would not endear them for long to adult society; but in adolescent company, where they are providers of enjoyable, 'status-providing' activities (Coleman 1961) they may find reward, and hence 'the cut off' is easily available, morally acceptable and self-rewarding.

Lackie (1962) suggested—discussing college athletes—that specific colleges attract students of similar characteristics and social outlook. The specialist colleges for physical education provide evidence in this country for an identical situation where those approximating towards a particular stereotype are accepted and acceptable. It would appear that on becoming teachers they continue a trend of traditional teaching. Limited by their own temperament and physique they transmit a value system of muscular achievement and success and a self-imitative philosphy (Smithells & Cameron, 1962).

Another possible danger is in terms of the reference group which was mentioned earlier in the chapter. Little clear-cut evidence exists on this point, though two recent investigations of the competitive swimming sub-culture (Hendry, 1967; Hendry & Whiting, 1968) have drawn attention to the risk of a closed conceptual system where the admired model serves as a motivation for those who are successful, and therefore, identified with the exemplar of the type, in turn imitates him and so perpetuates the system. Hendry (1967) wrote:—

It may be that swimming participation, admiration of the coaches' role and interests that fall mainly within the sporting scene predispose them to this kind of stereotyped response.

The study by Hendry & Whiting (1968) concluded that the high incidence of international standard junior swimmers (of whom a large percentage were selective school pupils) who proposed to become teachers of physical education suggested the possibility of a closed system in which the role of competitive success is over-valued. Hence there is evidence of a self-perpetuating, closed-conceptual system where often competitor becomes coach and, in turn, transmits an emphasis on certain values. It has been found that a large number of top class coaches had themselves swum competitively (Hendry 1968). The mechanisms for social control in this situation seems to be a rigid enforcement of work, achievement and success, so that the successes perpetrate the system. Here one can see possible links with the young athletes' aspirations towards a career in physical education where values are retained and, coupled with the personality of these teachers, innovation is difficult.

The existence of a particular stereotype within the teaching profession is also of interest because of the effect on the teacher's role. As has been explained earlier, but briefly, role theory enables those interested in the behavioural sciences to explain aspects of social inter-action in terms of status, role and expectations. Individuals approximate more or less to role stereotype—i.e. the expectations of others. The teacher's role, being involved in socialising tasks, the development of values, and 'child welfare', is diffuse. Nevertheless, the teacher of academic subjects carries certain 'main stream' subject specialisation, whereas the physical education teachers' role expectations are possibly concerned with children first, not subject-matter. Cannon (1964) in discussing the low status of women physical education teachers (in Direct Grant Grammar Schools) related to teachers of academic subjects, suggested that isolated physical education colleges start the process of alienation. Then, physical education is regarded as ancillary to normal school function, often utilising extra-curricular time. It is seen as a non-academic subject, and society still maintains vestiges of the puritanical notion of play. There is also the suggestion that the physical educationist is 'a man amongst boys' or 'a women amongst girls' and is thus, by definition, less mature than the rest of the staff. These factors may well lower perceived status (as reported by Appleby, 1967). Davies (1967) has intimated that the training of physical education students for their 'correct' function should consist of less emphasis on the personal physical skills development of students, and more on their preparation as educationists. With the possible existence of the described stereotype what can be achieved within the profession? Whitehead (1969) has indicated limited curriculum development, and existing psychological evidence would seem to suggest limited social reactions.

The two interacting factors or dimensions which affect social interaction are illustrated below (Getzels & Guba, 1957).

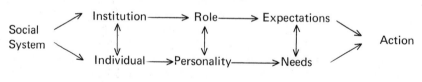

NOMOTHETIC DIMENSION

IDIOGRAPHIC DIMENSION

From this diagram it can be seen how role and personality affect each other, and how needs and other's expectations must be balanced out. The physical educationist then may well tailor his role in accordance with his temperamental predispositions, and resolve his needs in relation to the institution's view of 'the P.E. man'. It is fairly easy to speculate how, from historico-social beginnings the current stereotype of the physical educationist emerged.

Concluding Remarks

Is the apparently existing stereotypic image of the physical educationist a fairly accurate picture of this teaching fraternity?

Not only were the physical education students in Hendry's (1970) sample more muscular stable and extraverted than the general course students, but also more aggressive and competitive in their social responses. Further support was available from the Dynamic Personality Inventory scales where physical education students were shown to be verbally aggressive. Additionally, they were seen as being authoritarian, and submissive to strong authority—no doubt respecting this mode of dealing with people—this is mirrored in their attitude to teaching, which was more authoritarian than general course students. Yet they also revealed a number of characteristics which would make them attractive to young people—enthusiasm, sociability, activity, organisational abilities.

A conflict is apparent both for the physical educationist in achieving professional status amongst his staffroom colleagues, and also within himself in gaining his legitimate educational aims by over-riding his aggressive, attention seeking needs—allowing his social attractiveness to win positive attitudes towards the subject from an even wider range of pupils.

Physical education students liked the attention and admiration of others. They were seen as having a high achievement drive, and an eagerness to seek social roles. They had an interest in activity and physical adventure. There seems to be certain evidence here for the postulations of Sheldon & Stevens (1942) regarding the link between physique, temperamental and social traits, and to some extent the statements of Smithells & Cameron (1962) about the personality structure and social modes of the physical educationists' behaviour:—

> ... love of dominating, bold directness of manner, competitive aggressiveness ... (Carter, 1964),

and possibly a greater receptivity towards more skilled pupils with more immediate teacher-reward.

Carter (1964) somatotyped all staff members of one physical education faculty and found all of them to be mesomorphic. Thus there exists the possibility of a closed system where the stereotype is perpetuated.

Certainly few studies have been carried out on those who select physical education students—the college tutors. It may be appropriate to suggest that it would be useful to investigate such populations to ascertain the existence of a 'physical educationist' stereotype even in higher education. Another aspect of this finding is the actual product of the colleges. If there is a 'stereotype' of such dimensions as previously outlined then all the implications for teaching suggested by Smithells & Cameron (1962) may obtain, and the possibilities of a narrow role interpretation are apparent. Some attempt was made in Hendry's (1970) study to examine teaching effectiveness, but as the criterion used was the Institute's final teaching grade, which is really a predictor of ability, no clear-cut picture emerged about these postulated dangers.

Nevertheless, with the available evidence from this, and other recent studies (e.g. Jones, 1970), and consideration of Kane's (1968) findings that male and female physical education students are highly similar in personality structure, and unchanging in that structure across their three years of training, it may be pertinent for the physical education profession to consider whether or not the apparently existing 'stereotype' is an appropriate kind of teacher for future generations or whether the gates of the profession should open wide to allow a great variety of physical and temperamental 'types' to be admitted to specialist courses? Perhaps it may even be possible to suggest that the trend in 'the seventies' is going to be towards the gradual disappearance of the 'stereotyped' specialist as educational needs widen, and Davies (1967) has already pointed in this direction by suggesting that there should be less emphasis on the physical skills development of students, and more on their development as educationists. Of course a 'wind of change' in the shape of the B.Ed. degree is already blowing through the profession, although the effect and influence of physical education teachers with such qualifications in schools must await future investigations. It will be interesting to see how they are accepted in terms of status, and if they become more thoughtful, flexible innovative teachers. From Hendry's (1970) study, while suggestions must be tentative, it seemed apparent that the more permissive teacher of physical education was, in the eyes of his assessors, potentially the better teacher. This may be possible in terms of the creation of a warmer, friendlier, more informal approach, and the fact that as there is an association between personal qualities and effective teaching (Rhodes & Peckham, 1960).

In relation to staffroom colleagues and pupils, a subsequent study by Hendry (1971) has shown that the low status of the physical educationist is clearly perceived by other members of staff, and the status that does exist for the subject comes mainly from the success of sporting teams—the competitive elite of the school. Might this not reinforce the physical education teacher's need to give attention to the more highly skilled?

Nevertheless, all does not appear to be lost—despite the physical educationist's inclination towards this expectation of colleagues, at the possible expense of the educational needs of certain pupils; the teacher of physical education was considered by pupils to be a confidant and counsellor, a social educator, a 'pupil oriented' teacher and someone who truly had an interest in pupils as individuals. There is however a need to realise the wider recreative implications of the neglect of less able pupils.

Perhaps the profession should not be too paranoic in revealing educational deficiencies—for certainly no studies have probed the weaknesses and dissatisfactions of other subjects from a pupil-viewpoint—though of course awareness may be the first step towards innovation and improvement.

Whilst certain potential restrictions of teaching function may be embodied in the 'physical educationist' stereotype, these teachers have been shown to possess a number of qualities—enthusiasm, warmth and approachability, a liking for people, organising ability, and an enjoyment of the active, outdoor life—valuable in teaching the young.

Indeed, it must not be thought that this author perceives *all* physical educationists as conforming to the stereotypic characteristic described above, but rather that it has been a useful way of presenting evidence of the possible trends in teaching approach of physical education teachers.

Hendry's (1971) examination of the physical education teacher's role raises many pertinent questions about the school structure generally. For example, are the pressures of diverse expectations which impinge on the physical educationist also apparent in the other subjects which Musgrove & Taylor (1969) have grouped with physical education in a league table of status value within the teaching profession? It is suggested that along with physical education, music, art, domestic science and religious education are seen as marginal subjects. Marginality is present when a subject is not closely aligned to the instrumental, academic, examination geared purposes of the school.

In this situation it may not be surprising to find the physical educationist being 'pressed' towards the expectations of colleagues where status accrues from the success of sporting teams. This elitism may not necessarily be confined to physical education. As Hoyle (1969) has stated:

The teacher's role has been influenced by the elitist values pervading the education system, and on the whole has been committed to promoting the able rather than securing advance along a broad front.

The physical educationist may align himself to the expectations of staffroom colleagues rather than those of pupils, because as Musgrove & Taylor (1969) have reported the influence of the staffroom in England is very powerful indeed in terms of role reinforcement. The physical educationist who is concerned with only good physical performers may have his parallel in classroom teachers who coach the scholarship boys and cultivate only those showing academic potential. The physical education teacher who is polarised at the performance end of Parson's (1953) 'pattern variable' continua[5] might see himself in the role of a 'super coach' looking for potential from a mass of performers, selecting and working with certain individuals so that excellence of performance is the result.

Here certain links can be seen with Start's (1967) and McIntosh's (1966) findings that upper stream pupils (in the academic sense) are over-represented in school-teams. There seems to be little compensation for lower stream pupils within the competitive physical activities programme. Acceptance of school values or their rejection, and teacher-perceptions appear to be important considerations in this situation.

The implications of such upper stream reinforcement of superiority—in academic and sporting achievement—have been outlined by Hargreaves (1967) within a secondary school. He used such emotive, but no doubt accurate, terms as " 'warring' sub-cultures" in indicating the reaction of lower stream pupils in their attempts to gain some sort of parity with the higher academic streams in the sporting sphere of school-life. The dangers of maintaining an elite with regard to attitudes towards physical activities and post-school participation in leisure activities have also been pointed out (Hendry 1971).

The possible counselling role which was perceived by physical educationists, and suggested by pupils (if physical educationist could allow their obvious socially attractive qualities to emerge rather than their dominant, aggressive self-rewarding attitudes) may be a useful guide-line towards greater educational acceptance within the school, and an elevation of status for the subject in relation to classroom colleagues. The personality of the teacher, as well as his involvement in the 'expressive' sub-culture of the school, may be important factors in deciding whether physical education has a part to play in counselling and guidance. Once more the stereotypic dimensions of the physical educationist must be mentioned, because it would appear that the teacher himself must

---

[5]These continua are five polarised dimensions of behaviour which can be utilised to illustrate teaching dichotomies where role definition is needed. The position a teacher adopts on any behaviour continuum may indicate possible action.

resolve an inner conflict, and gain sufficient professional confidence to disregard the expectations of colleagues towards a sporting elite, to greater involvement in educational issues, to better salesmanship and belief in the values of his subject (Hendry 1971).

Nevertheless such a development as counselling could contribute towards a lessening of marginality, and perhaps enable the physical educationist to consider the wider dimensions of his role. Certainly the fact that physical education is completely non-examinable (the only school subject in this position) may be vital to this discussion, with varied situations and liberty from externally imposed schemes of work. That the teacher of physical education has no *direct* influence on life-chances of pupils may make him, as reported by pupils, the kind of teacher a boy could confide in, and approach in all sorts of problem areas (Hendry, 1971). Greater educational integration may be the way towards removal of the stereotypic image of the physical education teacher and a more successful realisation of legitimate educational goals.

References

ADORNO, T.W., FRENKEL-BRUNSWICK, E., LEVINSON, D.J. & SANFORD, R.N. (1950). "The Authoritarian Personality." New York: Harper.

AHMAVAARA, Y. (1954). Transformation analysis of factorial data. *Ann. Acad. Sci. Fenn.,* Series B. **88**, 54-59.

ALLPORT, G.W. (1961). "Pattern and Growth in Personality." New York: Holt, Rinehart & Winston.

APPLEBY, S.F. (1967). The role of the male teacher of physical education as perceived by men students in a college of education. Diploma Dissertation, Univ. Manchester.

BALE, P. (1969). Somatotyping and body physique. *Phys. Educ.,* **61**, 75-82.

BANKS, O. (1968). "The Sociology of Education." London: Batsford.

BELL, M. (1969). Personality factors in relation to educational gymnastics. M.A. Thesis, Univ. Sussex.

BOARD OF EDUCATION (1933). "Syllabus of Physical Training for Schools." London: H.M.S.O.

BRODSKY, C.M. (1954). A study of norms for body-form behaviour relationships. Cathol. Univ. of Am. Press, 1954. Cited in B.R. McCandless (1960) *Psychiat. Res. Rep.,* **13**, 42-57.

BROOKE, J.D. (1967). Extraversion, physical performance and pain perception in physical education students. *Res. Phys. Educ.,* **1**, 23-30.

CANNON, C. (1964). Some variations in the teacher's role. *Educ. for Teach.,* **64**, 29-36.

CARR, R. (1970). Personality traits of specialist (male) physical education students. Unpublished memorandum. Jordanhill College of Education, Glasgow.

CARTER, J.E.L. (1964). The physiques of male physical education teachers in training. *Phys. Educ.,* **56**, 66-76.

CARTER, J.E.L. (1965). The physiques of female physical education teachers in training. *Phys. Educ.,* **57**, 6-16.

CASSELL, R.N. (1963). "The Test of Social Insight." New York: Bruce.

CATTELL, R.B. (1946). "The Description and Measurement of Personality." New York: Yonkers.

CATTELL, R.B. & EBER, H.W. (1957). "16 Personality Factor Questionnaire." Champaign, Illinois: I.P.A.T.

COLEMAN, J.S. (1961). "The Adolescent Society." New York: Free Press.

COUTU, W. (1951). Role playing versus role taking: An appeal for clarification. *Am. Sociol. Rev.,* **16**, 180-187.

CURETON, T.K. (1951). "Physical Fitness of Champion Athletes." Urbana: Univ. Illinois Press.

DAVIES, H. (1967). The training of teachers of physical education. *Bull. Phys. Educ.,* Feb., 9-25.

DIBIASE, W.J. & HJELLE, L.A. (1968). Body image stereotypes and body type preferences among male college students. *Percept. Mot. Skills,* **27**, 1143-1146.

DUGGAN, A.S. (1937). A comparative study of undergraduate women, majors and non-majors in physical education, with respect to certain personality traits. *Res. Quart.,* **8**.

EDWARDS, A.L. (1953). "Edwards' Personal Preference Schedule." New York: Psychol. Corp.

ERANKO, O. & KARVONEN, M.J. (1955). Body type of Finnish champion lumberjacks. *Am. J. Phys. Anthrop.,* **13**, 331-344.

ESPENSCHADE, A. (1948). Selection of women major students in physical education. *Res. Quart.,* **19**, 70-76.

EVANS, F.J. (1967). Field dependence and the Maudsley Personality Inventory. *Percept. Mot. Skills,* **24**, 526.

EYSENCK, H.J. & EYSENCK, S.B.G. (1964). "Manual of the Eysenck Personality Inventory." London: University Press.

EYSENCK, H.J. (1947). "Dimensions of Personality." London: U.L.P.

EYSENCK, H.J. (1965). "Fact and Fiction in Psychology." Harmondsworth: Penguin.

EVANS, K.M. (1969). Teachers and some others: a comparative study. *Educ. Res.,* **11**, 153-156.

FLANAGAN, L. (1951). A study of some personality traits of different physical activity groups. *Res. Quart.,* **22**, 312-323.

FLEISHMAN, E.A. (1964). "The Structure and Measurement of Physical Fitness." New Jersey: Prentice-Hall.

GETZELS, J.W. & GUBA, E.G. (1957). Social behaviour and the administrative process. *School Rev.,* **65,** 423-441.

GRYGIER, T.G. (1961). "The Dynamic Personality Inventory." Slough: N.F.E.R.

HARGREAVES, A. (1968). Physical education in the Bachelor of Education degree. Diploma Dissertation, Univ. Keele.

HARGREAVES, D.H. (1967). "Social Relations in a Secondary School." London: Routledge & Kegan Paul.

HAVERLAND, E. (1957). 16 P.F. profile of teachers. In R.B. Cattell & H.W. Eber, "16 P.F. Handbook." Champaign: I.P.A.T.

HENDRY, L.B. (1967). Loughborough report. *Swimming Times,* **44.**

HENDRY, L.B. (1968). Assessment of personality traits in the coach-swimmer relationship, and a preliminary examination of the father-figure stereotype. *Res. Quart.,* **39,** 543-551.

HENDRY, L.B. (1969). Methods of student selection in male specialist colleges of physical education. Unpublished memorandum.

HENDRY, L.B. (1970). A comparative analysis of student characteristics. M.Ed. Thesis: Univ. Leicester.

HENDRY, L.B. (1971). An exploratory study of expectations for the physical education teacher's role. M.Sc. Thesis: Univ. Bradford.

HENDRY, L.B. & WHITING, H.T.A. (1968). Social and psychological trends in national calibre junior swimmers. *J. Sports Med. Phys. Fit,* **8,** 198-203.

HEATON, J. (1969). The role of the male physical education teacher working with boys in Secondary schools. Dip. in Educ. Thesis, Univ. Birmingham.

HOYLE, E. (1969). "The Role of the Teacher." London: Routlege & Kegan Paul.

HYMAN, H.H. (1960). Reflections on reference groups. *Public Opinion Quart.,* **24,** 383-396.

JONES, M.G. (1970). Perception, personality and movement charactertistics of women students of physical education. M.Ed. Thesis, Univ. of Leicester.

KANE, J.E. (1965). Personality profiles of physical education students compared with others. Proceedings of the First International Congress on Psychology of Sport, Rome.

KANE, J.E. (1968). Personality in relation to physical abilities and physique. Ph.D. Thesis, Univ. London.

KIKER, V.L. & MILLER, A.R. (1967). Perceptual judgement of physiques as a factor in social image. *Percept. Mot. Skills,* **24,** 1013-1014.

LACKIE, W.L. (1962). Personality characteristics of certain groups of inter-collegiate athletes. *Res. Quart.,* **33,** 566-573.

LEE, S.F. (1968). The role of the male teacher of physical education as perceived by men students following a main course in physical education at two colleges. Diploma Dissertation, Univ. Manchester.

LINTON, R. (1936). "The Study of Man." New York: Appleton-Century.

LOCKE, J. (1962). Performance of administration oriented male physical educators on selected psychological tests. *Res. Quart.,* **33,** 418-429.

MCCANDLESS, B.R. (1960). Rate of development, body build and personality. *Psychiat. Res. Rep.,* **13,** 42-57.

MCCLELLAND, D. et al (1953). The achievement motive. Cited in J.E. Hochberg (1964) "Perception." New York: Prentice-Hall.

MCINTOSH, P.C. (1966). Mental ability and success in school sport. *Res. Phys. Educ.,* **1,** 1.

MEAD, G.H. (1934). "Mind, Self and Society." Chicago: Univ. Press.

MEISSNER, A.A., THORESON, R.W. & BUTLER, A.J. (1967). Relation of self concept to impact and obviousness of disability among male and female adolescents. *Percept. Mot. Skills,* **24,** 1099-1105.

MILLER, A.R. & STEWART, R.A. (1968). Perception of female physiques. *Percept. Mot. Skills,* **27,** 721-722.

MUSGRAVE, P.W. (1965). "The Sociology of Education." London: Methuen.

MUSGROVE, F. & TAYLOR, P.H. (1969). "Society and the Teacher's Role." London: Routledge & Kegan Paul.

OLIVER, J.N. (1956). An analysis of the various factors associated with the assessment of teaching ability in physical education. *Brit. J. Educ. Psychol.,* **26,** 66-77.

PALMER, J. (1933). Personal qualities of women teachers of physical education. *Res. Quart.,* **4,** 4, 31-48.

PARNELL, R.W. (1958). "Behaviour and Physique." London: Arnold.

PARSONS, T. (1953). "Towards a General Theory of Action." Illinois: Free Press.

PERCIVAL, S.W. (1967). Physical education for what? Its role in the secondary school. *Phys. Educ.,* **59,** 1-9.

REPORT ON ENTRY TO COLLEGES OF EDUCATION (1967). Men accepted at colleges of education in Sept. 1966/Jan. 1967. London: H.M.S.O.

RHODES, F.G. & PECKHAM, D.R. (1960). Evaluation of beginning teachers: pointers and opinions. *J. Teacher Educ.,* **11,** 55-60.

SCOTLAND, J. (1964). The physical education teacher. *Scot. Bull. Phys. Educ.,* **1,** 2.

SHELDON, W.H., STEVENS, S.S. & TUCKER, W.B. (1940). "The Varieties of Human Physique." New York: Harper.

SHELDON, W.H. & STEVENS, S.S. (1942). "The Varieties of Temperament." New York: Harper.

SLEET, D.A. (1969). Physique and social image. *Percept. Mot. Skills,* **28,** 295-299.

SKINNER, B.F. (1953). "Science and Human Behaviour." London: Macmillan

SMITHELLS, P. & CAMERON, P.E. (1962). "Principles of Evaluation in Physical Education." New York: Harper.

START, K.B. (1967). The substitution of games performance for academic achievement as a means of achieving status among secondary school children. *Brit. J. Sociol.,* **17**, 300-303.

SUGERMAN, A.A. & HARONIAN, F. (1964). Body-type and sophistication of body concept. *J. Pers.,* **32**, 380-394.

SUTTON-SMITH, B. & ROBERTS, J.M. (1963). Games involvement in adults. *J. Soc. Psychol.,* **34**, 119-126.

TANNER, J.M. (1964). "The Physique of the Olympic Athlete." London: Allen & Unwin.

TAPPEN, N.C. (1950). An anthropometric and constitutional study of championship weightlifters. *Am. J. Phys. Anthrop.,* **8**, 49.

TAYLOR, P.H. (1965). Children's evaluation of the characteristics of a good teacher. *Brit. J. Educ. Psychol.,* **32**, 258-266.

THORPE, J.A. (1958). A study of personality variables among successful women students and teachers of physical education. *Res. Quart.,* **29**, 83-93.

WARBURTON, F.M. (1969). Personal correspondence. Faculty of Education, Univ. Manchester.

WELLS, W.D. & SIEGEL, B. (1961). Stereotyped somatotypes. *Psychol. Rep.,* **8**, 77-78.

WESTWOOD, L.F. (1967). Role of the teacher. *Educ. Res.,* **9**, 122-134 and **10**, 21-37.

WHITEHEAD, N.J. (1966). Education or training?—The hidden potential. Acad. Dip. Dissertation, Univ. Leeds.

WHITEHEAD, N.J. (1969). An examination of physical education programmes in men's colleges of education with relation to boys' physical education in secondary schools. M.Ed. Dissertation, Univ. Leicester.

WHITING, H.T.A. (1966). The personality profiles of male teachers of physical education. Unpublished memorandum, Univ. Leeds.

WILLGOOSE, C. (1961). "The Evaluation of Health, Education and Physical Education." New York: McGraw-Hill.

WILSON, B.R. (1962). The teacher's role—a sociological analysis. *Brit. J. Sociol.,* **131**, 15-32.

WITKIN, H.A., LEWIS, H.B., MACHOVER, K., MEISSNER, P.B. & WAPNER, S. (1954). "Personality Through Perception." New York' Harper.

WITKIN, H.A., GOODENOUGH, D.R., KARP, S.A., DYK, R.B. & FATERSON, D.R. (1962). "Psychological Differentiation." New York: Wiley.

AUTHOR INDEX

INDEX